# Is God Really There?

## ...and Is He Good?

## BILLY SPRAGUE

**HARVEST HOUSE PUBLISHERS**
Eugene, Oregon 97402

*Cover by Terry Dugan Design, Minneapolis, Minnesota*

## IS GOD REALLY THERE?

Formerly titled *Ice Cream as a Clue to the Meaning of the Universe*

Text copyright © 2002 by Billy Sprague
Published by Harvest House Publishers
Eugene, Oregon 97402

Library of Congress Cataloging-in-Publication Data
  Sprague, Billy.
    [Ice cream as a clue to the meaning of the universe]
    Is God really there? / Billy Sprague.
      p. cm.
    Originally published: c2000
    Includes bibliographical references
    ISBN 0-7369-0964-8
      1. Sprague, Billy. 2. Poets, American—20th century—Biography. 3. Gospel musicians—United States—Biography. 4. Christian biography—United States. I. Title.

  PS3569.P628 Z474 2002
  811'54—dc21
  [B]
                                                                    2001051700

**Printed in the United States of America**

  02  03  04  05  06  07  08  09  / BP-CF/  10  9  8  7  6  5  4  3  2  1

*This book is dedicated to*
*Kellie, my dear wife.*
*And to our children,*
*Willow Grace and Wyatt,*
*my muses with faces.*

# Acknowledgments

I am grateful to all the people who thought I had a book in me waiting to come out. Also to those who helped get it out. And special thanks to those who added to this effort from the manuscript of your lives.

Roberta Croteau, who has championed a way for me and others to write, and creates avenues to make that happen. My editors at Harvest House, Carolyn McCready and Terry Glaspey, for their affirmation, belief, and skilled guidance. Michelle Pruett Pottebaum, who years ago handed me a blank spiral notebook and challenged me to write. My longtime mates Jim Weber, Mike Nolan, Bill Sinclair, Greg Seneff, and Reed Arvin who help push dreams into the daylight. Wayne Kirkpatrick, for his partnership in songwriting and an artful heart that fuels the creative fires and friendship. Hardy Hemphill, for the ever-raised glass of enthusiasm and the beautiful piano arrangement of Willow's lullaby.

I also want to thank the publishers and songwriters who granted permission to quote from their songs and works. In particular, Jason Christian of Harvard University Press for his help with the poetry of Emily Dickinson.

Myrtle Payne, my grandmother, who reads over my shoulder now from heaven. And Bill and Oteka, dad and mom, who have always thought there is very little I couldn't do.

> **I have good hope that there is something after death.**
>
> PLATO

> **I can't see Him— but I absolutely know He is there!**
>
> OWEN MEANY
> (in John Irving's *A Prayer for Owen Meany*)

# Dear Reader,

I've lived long enough to know that sometimes dreams come true. And that sometimes nightmares do as well. All my life, without being aware of it, I have been gathering my own set of dreams and nightmares—together with a wide range of experiences and observations—so that I might make a case to my restless soul about the reality of a world beyond this one and the reality of a God who is in charge of it. And more and more along the way I've tried to keep my eyes and heart open for hints and revelations about what He might be like.

I suspect we are all involved in the same detective work. Most of the time it's a process of haphazard gleaning. A song overheard, a strangely familiar smell, or something we see triggers a memory, and for a few moments we take a brief mental pilgrimage back to an earlier time in our lives. Occasionally, our journey into the past is more deliberate, via reunions or therapy or writing.

Sometimes the memories are pleasant, other times quite painful. But from them we hope to gain meaning that can help us make better sense of our lives and satisfy the nagging questions we are almost afraid to pose...

Does God really exist? And if He does, what effect does that have on my day-to-day existence? Who am I in the grand scheme of things? And if there's a God, and if He is supposed to be good, how do I make sense of all the pain and hurt and suffering in this world? Not to mention the pain in my own life? Does God really care?

This book is, more than anything, an act of remembering—something which none of us can ever fully avoid. In fact, even more than science, philosophy, theology, or shopping, remembering may be the single act of searching we engage in most often. As Frederick Buechner put it in *A Room Called Remember,* choosing to remember is "a search to the truth of our own lives at their deepest and dearest, a search to understand, to hear and be heard."

So, who do I hope hears me? The skeptic (both out there and within me); the wounded (also out there and within me); and my children who can add daddy's rememberings to their own search for meaning.

Even as I set out to unearth these memories, as I laid them out before me and began connecting the dots to see what picture emerged, I understood that there would always be so much that I would never fully understand. (At some point life requires a leap of faith.) But I hoped to discover some pattern of evidence, like the familiar constellation of lights that guide a sailor home. I also knew that what drives me to play archaeologist on my life and the world around me is one aching desire: to get a sense that all along the long and winding way—in the glory and agony and all points in between—I have not been alone.

We are not alone.

If true, this single truth makes all the difference.

And isn't this the assurance we all want? That Someone really is listening when we pray? That He will carry us across the stormy seas? And that He cares?

We are not alone.

If something in these pages helps bring that assurance into focus or simply lightens your load, then this act of remembering will be even more meaningful for me.

Billy Sprague

# Contents

# 1

# Ice Cream as a Clue to the Meaning of the Universe

*How sweet it is!*

JACKIE GLEASON

AS A YOUNG BOY, I HAD a recurring dream that delighted and terrified me. Between the ages of five and ten, I must have dreamed this exact story several dozen times.

The setting I always assumed to be Holland because many of the people wore wooden shoes. Out in the countryside, built way off by itself, was a one-room hut with a thick, thatched roof—a scene right out of a Hans Christian Andersen tale. In the middle of the room stood a heavy, rough-hewn square table with short legs—like a living room coffee table. On it sat a large, white earthen crock full of ice cream.

The delightful part of the dream was this: The crock was charmed—how or by whom I never knew or even wondered—

but it remained full of ice cream day and night, no matter how many people came to eat out of it. And thousands came. From all directions. Every day, all day, people, mostly children, lined up, spoon and bowl in hand, to taste the delicious treat. The line stretched out of sight. No one pushed or shoved. The atmosphere was festive. The crowd patiently filed in the front door, filled a bowl from the crock, and went out the back door. Some sat on the grass eating and enjoying their ice cream. I could hear them laughing. Others headed back to wherever they came from. No one got fat either. Everyone knew that no one would go away unsatisfied and you could come back anytime, as many times as you wanted. What a great dream. At least to that point. (And not a surprising one. What kid doesn't crave unlimited delight?)

Over time, though, for whatever reasons, people lost interest. The lines grew shorter and shorter until no one came at all. As a result, the crock began to overflow. It poured out ice cream so fast that the entire countryside was covered in the sweet, cold lava. Panic broke out, and grownups and children all over the country were drowning and screaming and freezing in it.

I always woke up with a jolt at that point, in high anxiety, breathing like I had been running in my sleep and with such vertigo that I could feel the atoms in my body spinning.

To this day, I have a voracious appetite for ice cream. A passion for it. My collection of over 80 scoops (if it rains ice cream, I'm ready) includes designs spanning a hundred years. We host a yearly celebration at the beginning of the summer called The Annual Ceremony of the Golden Scoop. Dozens of friends gather to consume many gallons of homemade Mexican Vanilla, Strawberry, Malt Chip, Coffee, Lemon, Raspberry, Toffee Crunch, and, of course, Chocolate. (I have only a vague impression that the flavor in my childhood dream alternated between vanilla and chocolate.) Although I now have enough self-restraint (and a wife) to limit my intake, for health reasons, there have been periods in which I ate two or three half gallons per week. On a visit to Florence, Italy, I discovered gelato. It struck me as perfect symmetry that the land that spawned Michelangelo, da Vinci, Ferrari, and Sophia Loren should create the crème de la crème of ice creams. I ate it four or five times a day.

Until recently, I held on to a tongue-in-cheek rationale that my consumption of ice cream has helped save the world. As long as I kept eating lots of it, mankind was safe from another ice age. However, this whimsical sense of personal purpose not only doubled as a flimsy justification for self-indulgence and masked the nagging uncertainty of what, if anything, the dream meant, but it has also led me to what was right under my nose all the time, namely, ice cream as a clue to the meaning of the universe itself.

Was God (or, The Maker, as we ice cream lovers like to call Him) whispering to me at an early age? Or was it just my overactive imagination and pancreas? Was God dropping visual hints through parables in my sleeping head, to guide me through a universe at times so cryptic, so chaotic, where pain and pride eclipse the obvious? And was the same God who made a pack mule talk (Numbers 22) and put a gold coin in a fish's mouth to pay the local tax man (Matthew 17:27), in His wit and wisdom, giving me a cool, sweet, edible signpost on the way through this life?

To the skeptic I say, God gave Newton an apple as a clue to the laws of the natural universe. If an apple led to revelation of such magnitude, why not ice cream? To the atheist I say, pardon my presupposition of the existence of an active, interested, eternal being/designer behind a) the visible universe in general and b) the apple in particular that fortuitously fell on young Isaac's lunch break in Cambridge. Pardon me especially for presupposing a God before showing a just and rational cause to make such a leap (however short or long).

And to the modern naysayer I say, have a scoop of one of your own favorite virtues, openmindedness, and hear me out.

Now, you may say, all right, but what about those who were born and died before the advent of ice cream? First, I'm sorry they journeyed from birth to grave without the cool relief of Raspberry Sorbet or the languorous comfort of Chocolate Almond Fudge. Second, I'm not saying ice cream is the only clue to the meaning of the universe. I am interested in truth, not dogma. And truth breaks through in many ways. Each pilgrim in each age must have encountered his or her own clues to the mystery of creation and either read, misread, or missed altogether the revelation in them. I only know that for this pilgrim, Providence spotlighted this particular clue in a young boy's dreamscape.

(Does it not follow that a Clue-giver wants to be found out? Albeit indirectly, like poetry. Perhaps what (Who?) lies behind the universe is so inscrutable that it cannot be understood directly, and must be framed in a parable of time and space, matter and flavor, where beginnings, changes, and endings weave a vast symphony of reality that is itself the scrim of higher reality?)

FEW QUIBBLE WITH THE NATURAL physical law that for every effect there must be a cause. Skeptics, atheists, cynics, and believers generally agree on that. What, then, is the cause of ice cream? Here's where answers diverge. The French claim to be the first to actually add cream to the recipe. The Italians hail Marco Polo as the envoy to carry the concept back from China. Most concede that the Roman emperors were among the first on record to send slaves to the mountains for snow and shaved ice over which they poured various mixtures of fruits and juices.

HOWEVER, WORKING BACKWARD from any recipe, one soon reaches the a priori assumptions that have made us a species of stargazers and headscratchers. Where did the ingredients themselves come from? Has matter always existed within the spinning universe until the right molecules tumbled into alignment to create, on the one hand, cows consequently cream, cocoa beans therefore chocolate, sugarcane hence sugar, and chickens ergo eggs (or eggs ergo chickens), while on the other hand, brains to conceive, and opposing thumbs to construct mechanical devices for blending matter into a cool semi-solid to be savored by tastebuds that report to brains that trigger "oohs" and "aahs" of delight through lips that ask the eternal wherefore and why of it all?

Can such organization be random? It seems such a leap to assume intent inherent within matter alone. Yet many people make that leap of faith without hesitation, believing in "some dark and passing shadow within matter,"[1] as anthropologist Loren Eiseley described it in *The Immense Journey*. Can stones cry out absent an outside force to give them voice? "Without organization," wrote Eiseley, "life cannot persist."[2] Nor can ice cream. Nor any other created marvel. "It is obvious," he goes on, "that nature...has intentions and has made plans..."[3] In one breath he names this organizing force a "principle," while in another he says that somewhere in the dark chocolate sauce of primordial ooze (I added that part about chocolate sauce) "moved the eternal mystery, the careful finger of God"[4] to shape cows and cocoa plants and sugarcane and chicken eggs, and eventually, us, in His own flavor. What most scientists in their clinical objectivity call a principle, millions call God.

IS IT ANY GREAT LEAP to consider that the "careful finger of God" might project video parables into the electrochemical matrix of my grey matter, in the form of dreams? The brain is after all a multi-functional organ fashioned as much as an antenna as a place to hang a baseball cap. Finally, after many years, the revelation behind the parable of my childhood dream has dawned on me. And it is this:

Life is a journey toward eternal delight. It is a bittersweet recipe for a delicious future that first requires crushing, sacrifice, and dying. At all levels, atomic to cosmic, the universe is spinning. We are being turned and blended, prepared for eternity with The Maker in whose presence is a fountain of endless pleasures. And in that place, no one goes away unsatisfied, grows fat, old, or weary of sweet perfection. There will be a great and sweet reunion of loved ones sitting together on the soft grass. And there will be no fear of death. Here, for now, we may taste the diluted hint of the paradise frost that awaits us. There, we will savor fully even as we are fully savored. And in that place, you will taste the ice cream and the ice cream will set you free.

# 2

# Wake Up and
# Smell the Chaos

*Let no man despise the secret hints and notices*
*of danger, which sometimes are given him...*
*that they are certain discoveries of an invisible*
*world...we cannot doubt: and if the tendency*
*of them seems to be to warn us...why should we*
*not suppose that they are from some friendly*
*agent...and that they are given for our good?*

DANIEL DEFOE
*Robinson Crusoe*

YEAH RIGHT, YOU MAY be thinking. That first chapter is
the kind of over-tidy, under-examined, saccharine leap-of-faith
cosmology that would make any rational, "modern-thinking,"
what-you-see-is-all-you-get skeptic blow a fuse and want to
puke. Someone like Holden Caulfield, the gifted-in-sarcasm
star of Salinger's classic *Catcher in the Rye* might say, "Wake

up and smell the chaos. If you really want to know the truth about the world spend a little more time in the rye fields of oblivion where people actually go hurtling right over the cliff every day and nobody catches them."

*Hold on, Holden.* I never said life was tidy and totally comprehendible. Or that it wasn't dangerous. There's plenty of evidence to the contrary. Real evil. And suffering. And fear. Like my other childhood dream, which had nothing sweet about it.

AT LEAST TWO DOZEN TIMES, I dreamed we were on a family trip in our station wagon (usually the big black Pontiac). The dream always began on a moonless, overcast night. All five of us kids are in the car, my two sisters and I in the middle seat, both younger brothers in the back fold-up seat, Dad driving as usual, and Mom sitting up front, her head resting on a pillow against the passenger door. (In real life we drove like this many times from a day at the lake or on vacation or to Grandma Myrtle's house.) We are all drowsy or asleep. The hum of the highway and the sound of rushing wind come from Dad's open vent window. Smoke from his cigarette streams out of it. The headlights fight back the darkness ahead. It is cozy. Familiar. Safe. Until. We are all jolted awake by a loud popping thud like a tire blowing out. Dad starts weaving wildly down the road. Then I hear broken glass and Dad yelling, "Get down! Get down!"

To our right, less than a hundred yards through the blackness, a vehicle keeps pace with us on a parallel road. All I can see are its headlights and small bursts of light. Someone in that car or truck is shooting at us. Dad careens left and right and speeds up and hits the brakes, then floors it again to make us a harder target. My sisters are screaming. Mom is crying and shouting. We race through the night up and down hills and around tight curves, unable to shake the faceless shooter. Huddled down in the floorboard, we try futilely to brace ourselves from being thrown around the car. Tires squeal. The engine whines. Gunshots spit at us. Many miss. Some don't. Glass shatters. Bullets hammer through sheet metal. The panic goes on and on until Dad shouts something about turning off the headlights, and when he does, the road ahead disappears.

Always, at that same point, I woke up sweating under the suffocating darkness of my covers and, owl-eyed and gasping for air, threw them off.

All this nocturnal turmoil happened amid my wholesome and happy, if less than idyllic, childhood against the backdrop of shows like *Ozzie and Harriet, Father Knows Best,* and *Leave It to Beaver.* Even the steady glow of goodness radiating from Mayberry, USA couldn't keep this sludge of deep fear from seeping into my psyche. The culture and news reports of the day were not full of terrorists and massacres at schools, churches, airports, offices, and restaurants. Those were still years and decades down the road in the '80s and '90s. (The earliest one in my experience was the sniper on the University of Texas tower in 1967.) This was the late 1950s and early '60s.

Who or what was telegraphing to my dreaming brain such a dark level of random, violent badness as a potential player in the cosmos? I had no personal experiences of death or violence, though I had seen my share of Western shoot-'em-ups and some World War II movies. But back then, even those were depicted without visual wounds or even blood. There was no theatre of realistic violence and gore yet.

Even when death finally visited our own family, it wasn't that traumatic for me. Grandpa, A.R., died on his birthday, December 3, 1964. I remember crying hard at the funeral but only because it was probably the first time I ever saw my dad emotionally shaken. And my sisters were crying. So I did, too. A.R. was my dad's stepfather. His real dad died three months before he was born. A.R. wasn't a very close grandfather to me. He was quiet. Stoic. He was eighty-three. He rocked in his rocking chair and moved slowly, unlike my spry, feisty,

Grandma Myrtle, who ran races with us. I remember looking at his body in the coffin at church. He was the first dead person I ever knew. But not the last.

A.R. was old. Old people are expected to die. There was nothing evil in it. And besides, I had my dark dream long before he died. And before three boys in our neighborhood drowned trying to slide on an icy pond. That was a calamity, but not evil (unless you consider all death a result of evil in a broken universe where it was not the original intent of The Maker).

The first real evil that shattered my young heart came the day JFK was assassinated in Dallas. I realize now that I cried a new kind of tears that day. Tears of a profound awareness. Of evil. I mourned, with almost everyone else, an assault on goodness (even if that goodness was more perceived or partial than real or complete). That happened more than a year before A.R. died, but the dark dream had already appeared many times.

Despite the unsettling nature of the dream, I was not a sleepless, fearful child. I played and ran through the rye field of childhood oblivious to any cliff of imminent danger.

It could be that I passively succumbed to the same shining haze of youth and small town normality that enabled *The Andy Griffith Show* to beam optimism and well-being through the black-and-white television and only once address the death of Opie's mother. When Opie's pet turtle, Wilford, accidently got stepped on and killed (right in front of the ice cream parlor), Andy tried to help him deal with the loss by talking about what it was like when Opie's Ma died. Opie looked up at Andy and asked, "Who stepped on Ma?" But how she died? Or when? Who knows? Why didn't Andy or anyone else ever speak of her? I suppose it was material too heavy for a sitcom back then. (In a later episode, "Wedding Bells for Aunt Bee," Opie asks Andy, "Did you and Ma have that kind of love?" meaning a forever kind of love. In a tender, comforting moment, Andy replies, "Yes, son, we did.") Nowadays, so many TV shows focus entirely on calamity, violence, or evil. It's a wonder anyone can sleep at all.

Since that time, a lot of calamity and evil have cycled past. The murders of Robert Kennedy, Martin Luther King, Jr., and John Lennon. Earthquakes. Cancer. War. Massacres. Tornadoes. Car wrecks. Car bombs. Broken homes. Terrorist attacks. Funerals. No need to make a complete list.

Whoever or whatever slipped that sleep-shattering video-parable into the VCR of my mind, the waking hours of my life have revealed and confirmed the reality it forced on me: Evil is real. Calamity is real, too, but not always evil—just a hungry lion that must feed like gravity must embrace. Some calamity can be evaded. Death cannot. It must feed on every living thing. But it, too, is not always evil.

*Is that better, Holden? Some of life stinks. I know you can agree with that. But here's something else, "if you want to know the truth," as you were so fond of saying.* Goodness is real, too. And stronger than evil, but will take a severe beating along the way, maybe even get killed, but never permanently. Boy, does that sound sappy in a modern world or what? *I'll bet you think I think this because I grew up on John Wayne movies, where in the end the bad guys always get what they deserve, and the good guy gets the girl. Wrong. Let me tell you why I think this, if you really want to hear about it. But first, just so you don't think you're the only one in the cosmos who can smell the chaos...*

# 3

# Alone in
# the Cosmos

*My God, my God, why have you forsaken me?*

JESUS

I AM EIGHT AND A HALF. There is no school today because of the snow. Big snow. Twenty-seven inches. I dress to go outside and play. My two brothers and two sisters are either watching TV or sleeping in. I head out the carport door unseen by anyone. The world is frozen. The bright sun and snow blind me. Not a soul in sight. I round the far corner of the house to investigate the tunnels we dug twenty-four hours ago in a drift that the storm piled all the way to the roof. Three tunnels meet in the middle. I am excited to slide down and through to the other side. I plunge in.

What awaits me are two lessons—one in physics and one in life. When snow melts slightly and refreezes, it expands. It has. The tunnels have not. They have contracted overnight. I hit the icy Y-shaped intersection and pin myself, arms to my sides, eight feet in and nine feet under refrozen snow. I can't move forward or go back.

Claustrophobia is a gift my father has already given me and my brothers by holding us down in wrestling matches until we scream in terror to be released.

This white giant has no ears and no heart. I am stuck. I shout for help. My voice dies like a gnat's cry in a bale of cotton. I can't breathe. I do the only thing I can do. Panic. Cry. Struggle. Shout. Get mad. Furiously mad. The longest fifteen minutes of my childhood pass. Finally, enraged and desperate, I dig my toes in, wriggle forward past the junction, through the tunnel and out the other side into the bracing freedom of the winter air.

No one believes my wild account.

&#126;   &#126;   &#126;

I am eleven. Nearly twelve. I am hiking with seven or eight other Boy Scouts after a weekend campout. We are completing a requirement for a hiking merit badge—five miles with full gear. I am scrawny. Sixty-five pounds. My pack, sleeping bag, and tent must weigh thirty. The plan is that at the five-mile point, a truck will meet us to carry us on into town.

The truck arrives, but it's already loaded with gear and there are too many of us to make it in one trip. The guys begin to throw their gear on and then scramble for a place on the back of the pickup truck. Someone must wait for a second run. I am the runt. Naturally, I am elected. They leave some gear with me. The driver says he will send someone back to pick me up.

I stand there as they pull away. The guys laugh. One of them yells, "Eat cactus if you have to!" Just the day before, we learned that the red apples of the prickly pear cactus are edible as long as you peel them carefully to remove the fuzzy, nearly invisible, and deadly thorns. I watch the truck until it is a smudge of dust on the dry Texas prairie.

Great. It's hot. Midday. The bright sun forces me to squint. I'm tired. So I collapse in the dirt to wait. The first hour I throw a lot of rocks. The second I watch the horizon and worry. The third I begin to be afraid and start hiking with all my gear. I don't really know the way back to town. I only know which way the truck headed. Town is at least twenty, maybe thirty, miles. The gear gets heavy. I drag the tent by a rope for a while and then leave it behind in the middle of the dusty road. And I begin to cry. In the fourth hour, I start to wonder if anyone knows where I am. How could they do this to me? No one is going to come for me, and I'm going to die out here. I really believe I am going to die. I begin to look for prickly pear apples but imagine swallowing some of the tiny thorns and dying in agony. There are none in sight.

The rugged plains are huge and empty. The sky is even bigger. I am sixty-five dusty pounds of anger, hurt, and tears. They'll feel bad when they find my dried body out here in a few days. And it serves them right! But that isn't the worst of it—dying, I mean. The real pain is being left behind and forgotten.

The sun sinks lower and lower. And so does any hope of survival. So this is it. I don't know God or much about Him. He seems as indifferent to my situation as my scoutmaster.

I keep walking. Crying. A few times, I shout. It's so quiet. Empty. I keep walking.

The sun goes down. It's not quite full dark when I see a moving light a long way off. It appears and then disappears. Comes closer. Headlights. I start to pick up my pace and then decide to play it cool. I wipe my eyes and face. The pickup truck stops. The driver tells me to get in. He tells me everybody got their wires crossed and assumed someone else had come to get me. I sulk and pretend to be OK, but I'm not. We retrieve the tent and drive back to town in silence.

∽ ∽ ∽

I am fourteen. I am standing outside by the gym at school just after lunch. My girlfriend comes over to me. Her name is Amy. She is a natural beauty. Blonde. Lives in the country. She has worn my ring for six weeks. She hands it back to me. *But why?* I had called her maybe twice in those six weeks. I'm too scared to talk. Every time I tried to dial the number, I could never finish. What would I say? So I never called.

"OK, Amy. I understand," I tell her. But I don't.

∽ ∽ ∽

I am fifteen. Water-skiing with some friends. I don't like skiing that much because my legs are so skinny and weak, and the boat driver always wants to go too fast. I fall. They see me fall. The boat keeps going. My friends are laughing as they round a point and disappear from sight. Nice joke. The first five minutes I expect them to reappear. The next five minutes I am angry. The next ten minutes I am certain another boat will run over me. I could swim to shore but I have no shoes. No other boats appear. The sky is huge and empty. The sun glares on the water. It is quiet except for my breathing and splashing as I turn in circles to watch for other boats. My "friends" finally return. "Thanks guys." Then I am quiet. Angry. But pretend to be OK.

∽ ∽ ∽

I am nearly sixteen. June. Earlier in the spring, I lost my virginity. Now I have found God. I am sitting alone on top of a picnic table under the stars at church camp. I am a sinner. Crying. The sky is black and huge. The night is so still. Millions of stars and not one twinkles. These words go round and round my brain: *I will never leave you or forsake you. You are Mine. I am with you even to the end of the age.* I want it to be true more than anything.

∽   ∽   ∽

I am nineteen. September. A nurse gives me a shot. Two orderlies transfer me to a gurney. They wheel me down a corridor of bright lights. I have been diagnosed with scoliosis, deteriorating curvature of the spine. "There was a crooked man who walked a crooked mile..." and he is me. When I wake up from this back surgery (if I wake up), I must spend nine months in a body cast. A plaster cocoon. My friends have all gone back to college. I will miss a year of school. Gestating. Incubating through the bitter West Texas winter. Long walks alone. Learning to play the guitar. Reading the New Testament from beginning to end for the first time. Under the bright lights, I wonder why God doesn't impress the doctors by healing me instantly. I am very sleepy. I tell Him He still has time. I wake up in heavy pain. The doctors were not impressed. Several days later, they wrap my torso in plaster up to my neck. "There was a crooked man..."

∽   ∽   ∽

I am twenty-three. I am standing in a carport at the back door of a townhouse. It is a scorching-hot summer day. My girlfriend's car is parked by his. He is rich, divorced, nearly twice her age—a "friend" to us both. I hesitate to knock, then decide to go quietly on in. As I sneak through the kitchen into the living room, all my suspicions are confirmed. They are on the couch. It's obvious where they are headed. I startle them. He pushes me back into the kitchen where we pursue a tense confrontation. Then he shoves me out the kitchen door. The sun blazes down. I drive away in a burning rage that smolders for five years.

～  ～  ～

I am twenty-four. Friday night. The manager of the pizza place where I sing and play guitar meets me at the door as I arrive. "Let's take a walk," he says. The president of the company likes Country & Western music. He doesn't consider The Eagles' music Country & Western. The manager has to "let me go." "Fired" is the word he works hard to avoid.

～  ～  ～

I am twenty-five. I am setting up a picnic beside a lake on a windy, cloudless afternoon. The charcoal glows in the grill. Drinks, ice, hot dogs, and all the fixins await the arrival of the kids from the church where I am the summer youth director. I wait. The first hour I triple check everything to see if it's in order. The second hour I chalk up to teenage tardiness. The third hour I begin to eat. No one shows. I take the afternoon off and eat hot dogs for a week.

～  ～  ～

I am twenty-nine. I am sitting on a cement bench. It is a sunny fall day. A young woman I love is telling me in the kindest way that she is marrying another man. Only last spring she had heard from God that I was to be her husband. Is she saying the voice she actually heard was the clamor of her own dreams and hormones? I remain calm, anesthetized by her tenderness, and receive the scalpel without a peep. I don't know what to say. The leaves float down from the trees.

∼ ∼ ∼

I am thirty-two. I am standing at a urinal at a Canadian border station. It is a clear, cold winter day. Finishing my business, I hurry out to find that our tour bus has vanished down the highway, oblivious to the fact that I am not aboard. A real Canadian Mountie and I overtake the bus in his car with lights flashing. I reboard the bus. No one knows I was missing.

∼ ∼ ∼

I am thirty-seven. Tuesday. I am twenty-five feet under water in rough seas off the Florida Keys. Visibility is poor, and the swells are strong. After a brief preoccupation with some formation, I turn to discover that both my dive buddies have disappeared. I attempt to retrace our course but become disoriented. Am I lost or are they? For about seven or eight minutes I am alone in the ocean. Anything can happen.

Saturday morning. Four days later. I am at thirty thousand feet somewhere over eastern Oklahoma looking at the earth below. Visibility is excellent, and the ride is smooth. Five miles down and one state over in southern Missouri, my bride-to-be is killed by a Ford pickup truck. I land in a different world than the one I took off from.

~ ~ ~

I am thirty-seven. Collapsed in the dirt beside the grave of my fiancée. The setting sun is in my face. The air is still. She has been dead almost four months. She was a natural beauty. Dark brunette. Green eyes. I am one hundred and sixty-five pounds of dust, anger, hurt, and tears. I know God, not fully, but in a personal way, as they say. I have read His Book. I have tried to walk in His ways. But I am a crooked man. God seems even more oblivious (or is He more sensitive?) to the situation than those who send well-intentioned but vacuous cards that contain poor poetry like, "Tears cannot come nor sorrow stay/ With Thy grace filling me...I only know a peace within/ For my loved one dwells with Thee." Tears cannot come? By grace they cannot be contained! I do not pretend to be OK.

My friends (those brave enough to leave the house of feasting and come to a house of mourning) tell me many are praying for me and that I am deeply loved. I know this is true. And it's some comfort and no doubt a strength beyond my awareness. But they also tell me I am not alone! What a lie. It is only a poor spiritual/semantic sleight-of-hand trick they have learned from others as awkward as they (or perhaps as fearful of being alone themselves). Make no mistake. I am alone. There are moments when life leaves us totally alone. Why are we so reluctant to admit that? We inhabit a crowded but lonely planet.

The huge sky reddens. Occasionally I speak aloud. To her. To God. Otherwise it's so quiet here. She is dead. But why? Someone got their wires crossed? I am a crooked man? But that's not the worst of it. The real pain is being left behind and forgotten.

I am in a frozen tunnel. This time, stuck for two years. Arms pinned to my sides. I can't breathe. I do what I can. Shout for help till I lose my voice. Cry. Struggle. Get mad. Furiously mad. I need help to get out of this one.

I am tired. My stomach feels like it's full of prickly pear cactus apples, unpeeled. And these words go round and round in my head: "I will never leave you nor forsake you. You are Mine. I am with you even to the end of the age." Now, more than anything I want that to be true. I *need* it to be true. If it is not, then I am truly alone...we are all truly alone...and beyond consolation.

# 4

# Almost Everything I Need to Know I Learned from the Andy Griffith Show

*I'm from a generation Lost In Space*
*Badly in need of some amazing grace*
*The TV took my babysitter's place*
*  Talk about a talking head*
*I was an Outer Limits episode*
*You were a signpost in my Twilight Zone*
*When you came whistlin down that country road*
*  Livin' every word you said*
*On CNN you get the same old news*
*On MTV they got the same old blues*
*I'm channel surfin for a different view*
*  There it is in black and white*
*A place where neighbors treat each other kind*
*The kind of place you always hope to find*
*And maybe Mayberry is on my mind*
*  Cause I still need a guiding light*

I GREW UP IN FRONT OF A TELEVISION. Until music captured my attention, TV probably influenced my early worldview more than any other single thing. Certainly more than John Wayne movies. I didn't read much, or like to, until college. (The only book I ever finished in high school was *A Tale of Two Cities,* which first convinced me reading could be more engaging and enjoyable than sitcoms and variety shows.) We didn't attend church early on, at least not regularly. So television was my main window on the world. And the world's main link to me.

Before color TV came in, it was a black-and-white world. To a kid like me, people on TV, and in real life, were either good or bad, not varying degrees of dysfunctional. We were good. The Russians were bad. We believed in God. They did not. Every now and then the Emergency Broadcast System's logo appeared on the screen, disrupting the benign spell cast by the tidy black-and-white worlds of *The Adventures of Ozzie and Harriet, Leave It to Beaver,* or *Father Knows Best.*

I vaguely remember a few air-raid drills in elementary school—another irritating intrusion of the cold war. When the hall bell would ring in a certain pattern, we knew to crouch by or under our desks with our hands on top of our trusting, obedient heads. (Nothing protects you from a nuclear blast quite like a school desk.)

Roy Rogers always foiled the bad guys. The "Beave" said "Yes, Sir," "Yes, Ma'am," and "Gee, Wally." He cleaned up his room and always learned his lesson. And Walter Cronkite, the reliable, no-nonsense news anchorman (not celebrity), told us how things were every day.

I'm sure the enlightened psychologists of this dawning millennium can trot out a long list of the dysfunctions, stereotypes, and politically-incorrect attitudes 40 years ago at 522 Sycamore Road in Hillsdale, USA—home of the Nelsons, and at 211 Pine Street in Mayfield, USA—congenial home of the Cleavers, and at 607 South Maple Street in Springfield, USA, where the Andersons of *Father Knows Best* lived. (Is it more than a coincidence that the Simpsons also live in Springfield? And Homer, the head of the house, portrays a "Father Knows Squat"?)

Granted, early TV presented a severely edited, partial view of human nature and the world, but it was cleaner and kinder, and the values were not as yet altered or "evolved" (blurred or eroded, many would say) by the '60s and '70s counterculture revolution.

Without realizing it at the time, I was basking weekly in the soft glow of the worldview from the front porch at 411 Elm Street, Mayberry, North Carolina via *The Andy Griffith Show*. This panorama included a simple joy, and humor, in living. Respect and care for others. A strong sense of justice and fair play. A high regard for honesty (except when it hurt someone's feelings or helped further the plot). A keen nose for arrogance and phoniness. Uncluttered meanings about friendship, loyalty, family, and duty. The residents of Mayberry shared a common affirmation and purpose for life, which was tied to an uncamouflaged belief in and reverence for God. In several episodes, Andy and Barney even harmonize a gospel tune. One was "Let the Lower Lights Be Burning."

> Brightly beams our Father's mercy
> From his lighthouse evermore
> But to us he gives the keeping
> Of the lights along the shore
>
> Let the lower lights be burning
> Send a gleam across the wave
> Some poor fainting, struggling seaman
> You may rescue, you may save.
> By Philip P. Bliss 1871 (public domain)

They have sure kept the lower lights burning and television sets glowing. The show has been on the air uninterrupted in syndication since its last episode aired September 16, 1968.

In the original opening to the show, Andy and Opie come walking, fishing poles in hand, down a dirt country road, beside a lake. Opie stops to throw a rock in the water, then runs to catch up with his Pa. (In the early episodes, he stopped again to throw another rock, but the second throw was later edited out to shorten the show from twenty-five to twenty-two minutes. Can you guess why? To cram in more advertising, of course.) The final camera shot of the opener shows the second rock hitting the water and the ripples spreading out around it.

For years, those ripples reached me at 207 Ozmer, in Borger, Texas. Decades later, they still do. They wash over me like the memories of actually fishing with my own dad, who, on one occasion, woke me up long before dawn from a crowd of sleeping cousins and brothers littered on a cabin floor in Riudosa, New Mexico. I heard him whisper, "Bill, get up, we're going fishing." I told him I'd wake up my two brothers, but he said, "No, just you and me."

We headed out to Lake Bonita, which means "beautiful lake." And it was. The mist still clung to the mirrored surface. Every tree stood reverently still. The lake had been freshly stocked with trout, and we hauled them in and laughed out-loud because, for that shining moment, the only thing below the surface of our lives, besides hungry rainbow trout, was the clear, deep water of the love between father and son. The ripples of that memory still reach me.

That fishing experience did not create the love between my dad and me. It only reflected and strengthened what was already there. In the same way, did the early cathode rays from Mayberry create my worldview or just reflect and reinforce things that were already inside me?

THIS GOES TO THE HEART of a controversy, voiced by John Locke in 1690 and then shifted into high gear by Jean-Jacques Rousseau (among others) in the 1700s. He popularized Locke's idea that at birth we're each an empty slate, tabula rasa, carrying no abstract information. On this "blank slate," systems and worldviews are written entirely by environment and life experience, by family and culture.

If so, is one belief system or worldview any clearer or better than another? Do we start with only an operating system of brain and neurons, or is information encoded on our genetic hard drives that starts us all out with certain givens? Do we come from the factory with a conscience? A moral compass? Eternal awareness? ("He [God] has also set eternity in the hearts of men," Solomon wrote in Ecclesiastes 3:11.) Or are these things, and more, installed like software by outside influences? Were Andy and Barney just crooning a tune from their childhoods? Is the perky musical opening to the show merely whistling in the dark? Any reason to keep the lower lights burning? Other than pure safety and social order? Certainly not, if the Divine lighthouse is empty and its keeper gone away, or more likely, *is* merely an archaic, mythical influence foisted on more enlightened generations by *our* superstitious, more simple-minded ancestors?

When I met Holden Caulfield in the Cliffs Notes to *The Catcher in the Rye* in the late '60s (I didn't read the whole book until college), I could tell right away he was not raised on sitcoms. (Maybe that's because he was already grown before TV really took off. Salinger first published *Catcher* in 1951.) His worldview is harsh and cynical. He is restless and perturbed, like someone is constantly scraping fingernails across his inner slate. (He needed a fishing trip with his dad real bad, but they might have drowned each other.)

However, on a closer look, Holden holds many of the same values as the simple citizens of Mayberry. Well, at least some of the values. OK, nearly four. A strong sense of justice (and injustice). A high regard for honesty (or at least the burly, no-neck cousin of honesty, bluntness). A low tolerance for phoniness. And a clear purpose, or at least aspiration, for life.

Holden wanted to grow up to be someone who stands in a big field where children are playing, oblivious to a nearby cliff, and all day long, as they come running by, he rescues them from falling off. A "catcher in the rye" he called it. That sounds a lot like a person who keeps the lower lights burning for sailors lost at sea, but in a field for at-risk children, instead.

Where did Holden (or any of us) get a sense of justice? From his dad, the lawyer? What gave him a nose for phoniness? Or the vision of what he wanted to be?—a protector and rescuer of children. Did it merely spring haphazardly from misremembered words of the Robert Burns poem? The line is supposed to be, "If a body *meet* a body coming through the rye." Not "catch" a body.

This is a classic picture of the debate between nature or nurture as the dominant influence on us. Is justice built into us or trained in? C.S. Lewis, in his chapter "Right and Wrong as a Clue to the Meaning of the Universe" (from the book *Mere Christianity*) makes the case that it's built in and, *as such,* is evidence pointing to the existence of God. B.F. Skinner and other behavioral scientists make the opposite case, believing, like Rousseau, that environment and training produce our sense of right and wrong.

More than 30 years before either C.S. or B.F. was born, Dostoyevsky conducted a grand, fictional experiment in *Crime and Punishment*. The main character, Raskolnikov, deliberately steps outside his moral culture by committing a murder, confident that some men—exceptional men—are not limited by the same boundaries as are the masses. (In the next century, Hitler tested this assumption on a grander, more catastrophic scale and millions of real, not fictional, people died.) The police inspector, Porfiry, patiently and doggedly pursues Raskolnikov, convinced that, try though we may, we cannot escape our human nature universally wired within us. The author's conclusion? We are encoded with moral awareness, and we ignore it at our own peril. Our sins will find us out. Sure enough, the weight of guilt drives Raskolnikov to confess. He is convicted and sent to Siberia, where, in prison, he finds freedom through forgiveness in Christ.

But where did Dostoyevsky get his viewpoint of human and spiritual realities? Did someone write that on his heart and mind as a child? (Some Andy Griffithsky? Impossible. The Russians are the bad guys, remember?) Or did the story emerge from and reflect the universal sense of crime and justice, sin and atonement, in us all?

In 1989, 123 years after the first publication of *Crime and Punishment*, the quirky filmmaker/philosopher Woody Allen turned Dostoyevsky's concept upside down in a movie called *Crimes and Misdemeanors*. In Allen's version, Judah, a middle-aged, successful eye doctor, reluctantly pays to have his mistress killed before she can expose the affair to his wife. In a crisis of conscience, Judah consults his rabbi who offers, among other thoughts, these lines: "It's a fundamental difference in the way we view the world. You see it as harsh and empty of values and pitiless, and I couldn't go on living if I didn't feel with all my heart, a moral structure, with real meaning, and forgiveness, and some kind of higher power, otherwise there's no basis to know how to live!" But in typical Allen style of turning a worldview on its head, Judah wrestles with his guilt and manages it, saying, "God is a luxury I can't afford." Absolving himself, he goes on with his unsuspecting wife and his life, unconvicted legally or morally. Evil is rewarded. Good is punished.

Woody Allen painted a dark picture of a twentieth-century phenomenon—the moral evolution (moral-ectomy, some would say) of the human psyche. Can the inner tablet be over-written or re-etched to accommodate moral misdemeanors and atrocities without any shame or guilt? (Unfortunately, a view of the conscience as optional, like the appendix, is growing in popularity. Fortunately, when asked, "What do you want to be when you grow up?" most kids, even angry, cynical kids like Holden Caufield, do not consider "sociopath" an honorable life pursuit.)

On a broader scale, can human nature be reshaped, re-engineered into an updated, more streamlined model, better suited for life in the fast-lane future?

In 1931, Aldous Huxley described what a nurture-dominated world might look like in the novel *Brave New World*.

It is set in the year A.F. 632, which stands for After Ford, meaning Henry Ford, the industrialist who developed mass production techniques. Babies no longer arrive the usual way, but are incubated and "decanted" from bottles. A sorting and conditioning process at the fetal and infant stages predetermines all levels of society, from unskilled labor on up. This includes neo-Pavlovian use of alarms and sirens to make infants fear books and roses (which represent free thought and beauty—elements historically very destabilizing to society). Sleep-teaching, the constant repetition of recorded ethical phrases, is used to saturate the subconscious with the desired values of the New World Order. Divisive institutions like religion and monogamy have been eradicated. Long-term relationships are discouraged. (Not a real sitcom scenario, is it? Unless you put it in Woody Allen's hands, which birthed the movie, *Sleeper*, 1973.)

One of the main characters, Bernard Marx, a small, dark-haired, independent-thinking man with an inferiority complex, defies the training and rules that society has engineered, simply by falling in love. Eventually, he and another character, who rocks the boat by writing a poem about being alone, are exiled to an island for social misfits.

One of Huxley's points is very clear: There is something in the human critter that makes him more than a critter. You may genetically and socially tinker all you like, but the human "spirit," for lack of a more scientific word, will break out and persist in showing certain characteristics that were supposed to be edited out or redirected by all the elaborate engineering. Huxley's imaginative *Brave New World* is a long way from Mayberry, USA.

IMAGINE AN EPISODE of *Andy Griffith* where B.F. Skinner's car breaks down on his way back to Harvard for an important lecture titled, "Pavlov's Dogs as a Clue to the Messiness of the Universe." On the same day, Aldous Huxley arrives to defend his book, which the library has banned (along with *The Catcher in the Rye*). There is a protest in progress on Main Street led by the well-meaning but nosy neighbor, Clara Edwards, and Floyd, the barber. Helen Crump, the school teacher, is the lone advocate for the books. And, for a touch of irony, Deputy Barney Fife, a small, dark-haired, independent-thinking man with an inferiority complex, locks up young Woody Allen for littering and graffiti. (Barney caught him spray painting on the side of Weaver's Department Store—"Homer Simpson will steal my paranoia.")

Skinner is flustered and adamant about repairing the car and traveling on, but Wally's station is closed. Andy reconditions his response with Aunt Bee's pot roast and apple pie and persuades him to spend the night so Wally can fix his car in the morning. Mr. Huxley has already been taken to 411 Maple to protect him from the angry mob. After supper, Andy, Aunt Bee, Barney (Huxley calls him Bernard), Dr. Skinner, and Aldous ("Al," Barney calls him) retire to the front porch.

After a lively, sometimes heated, discussion between Skinner and Huxley about history and education and epistemology (which Barney explains to Andy is the study of pistols), Andy reaches for his guitar saying, "Around here, some things you just know." And before either guest can contradict or "hold forth" any more, Andy and Barney launch into a song:

> Play Fair—Work Hard
> Look for Happiness in your backyard
> Make Peace—Laugh Loud
> Keep the Faith that's what it's all about
> And whatever you do Be Yourself…and Love Well

"Love Well" © 1999 Mail Train Music/ Skin Horse, Inc (ASCAP) by Phil Madeira and Billy Sprague. Used by permission.

Opie enters through the screen door in his jammies and says, "Goodnight, Mr. Skinner. Goodnight, Mr. Huxley, thanks for the swell book. Night, Barney. Night, Aunt Bee. Goodnight, Pa." Andy pats his son on the shoulder and says, "Goodnight, Ope." Opie exits.

"You've trained him well," says Skinner.

Huxley adds, "That boy's got a bright future ahead of him."

Barney confirms it in a knowing tone, "Yeah, the future is ahead of him, alright."

Andy smiles and puts it simply. "He's a good boy. Gets it from his mother." And then leads Bernard right into the next refrain:

> Shoot Straight—Be Square
> When somebody needs a hand Be There
> Slow Down—but Don't Quit
> What you make of life is what you get
> And whatever you do Be Yourself...and Love Well
> "Love Well" © 1999

(Fade to black. Segue to theme song and credits as Skinner and Huxley argue about where Opie's goodness comes from.)

IN REALITY, MOST REASONABLE people agree that nature and nurture are both powerful shapers of who we are. Growing up, Holden got a lot more of New York City than I did. And I got a lot more Mayberry. I enjoy visiting New York City; in fact, I grew up watching Mickey Mantle and Roger Maris swat 'em out of the park. I'm a lifelong Yankee fan. Call me a "stick in the mud," but I'd rather stick with Andy Griffith than swap places with Holden Caulfield for any new worldview, brave or otherwise.

> To Otis & Howard, Gomer & Floyd
> Charlene and the music of the Darlin boys
> To Wally & Goober, Ernest T Bass
> And sweet Aunt Bee, with all her down home class
> To Helen Crump and Thelma Lou
> The Mount Pilot girls and little Opie, too
> To Sheriff Andy Taylor, and One-Bullet Barney Fife
> To one and all my hat is off tonight
> "Love Well" © 1999

# 5
# How Sweet the Sound

*After silence, that which comes nearest to expressing the inexpressible is music.*

ALDOUS HUXLEY

MY EARLIEST MUSICAL MEMORIES are, not surprisingly, children's songs. The birth of my own children revived them (re-released them as they say in the music business). "Twinkle, twinkle, little star/How I wonder what you are." "Rockabye Baby." "Row, row, row your boat gently down the stream/ Merrily, merrily, merrily, merrily, life is but a dream." "Jesus loves me." "Mary had a little lamb." "Ring around the rosy." "You are my sunshine." And one of my personal favorites because of its nonsense wordplay, the old counting song:

> This old man, he played one
> He played knickknack on my thumb
> With a knickknack, paddywhack
> Give your dog a bone
> This old man came rolling home.
>
> (composer unknown—public domain)

(What is the game of knickknack, anyway? And even if you do give your dog a bone, hasn't "paddywhacking" been outlawed by the SPCA?)

For some reason, I remember especially my mother singing this one:

> I see the moon and the moon sees me
> Down through the leaves in the old oak tree
> Please let the light it shines on me
> Shine on the one I love
> <small>(composer unknown—public domain)</small>

I also sing a few songs to my little ones that I've written for them. One is from a long time ago when I was only dreaming about having children called "Dream a Dream" (see Chapter 10, Memos to the Almighty). And this one, also a bedtime song, arrived after my first child, Willow Grace, was born.

> Where do I, Where do I
> Go when I'm afraid?
> Who is there, Who is there
> Listening when I pray?
> How can I, How can I
> Cross a stormy sea?
> My heavenly Father is
> Watching over me
>
> Sail away, Goodnight
> Sail away, Goodnight
> Sail away, Goodnight
> Sail away, Goodnight
> <small>"Sail Away" © 1998 Skin Horse, Inc. (ASCAP)<br>by Billy Sprague. Used by permission. All rights reserved.</small>

The soundtrack to my childhood was a collage of the recordings my mother listened to, like Sinatra singing "Young at Heart" from the album *This Is Sinatra*, Dean Martin crooning "That's Amore," musicals like *The King and I*, *The Music Man*, and from *My Fair Lady*, songs like "I Could Have

Danced All Night." She had the Mills Brothers' greatest hits, including "Paper Doll" and "Lazy River," and the Eddy Arnold album *My World* with the song "Make the World Go Away." I remember thinking how warm and sad his voice was. Mom often sang the chorus to Doris Day's "Que Sera Sera" around the house.

The big stereo console in the living room automatically dropped a series of records, so that over the span of several hours, I might head out into the yard to the tune of "Sixteen Tons" by Tennessee Ernie Ford, pop back in for a snack with accompaniment by Louis Armstrong, and waltz back outside to Johann Strauss.

In my mind, I can still see the jackets to some of those records. One was called *The Stars Sing for Children of all Ages.* Against a white background were about ten stars. In each star was a face and below it the person's name and the title of a song on the record. Bing Crosby—"Never Be Afraid"; Captain Kangaroo—"Button Up Your Overcoat"; Jimmy Durante—"I Like People"; Roy Rogers—"Hoofbeat Serenade"; Cab Callaway—"Minnie the Moocher"; and Burt Parks singing my personal favorite, "Skidamarink-A-Dink" (means I love you).

I especially remember hearing a lot of Nat King Cole. Songs like "Embraceable You" and "Mona Lisa." I didn't have any idea who Mona Lisa was but I knew she had to be some kind of beautiful to have a song like that written about her. The record of his that Mom played most was *Everytime I Feel the Spirit.* I knew which song was coming next before it began. It included "I Want to Be Ready," "Sweet Hour of Prayer," "Oh, Mary Don't You Weep," "Go Down Moses," "Nobody Knows the Trouble I've Seen," and "In the Sweet By and By." I still love the way Nat sang the word "shall" in the line "We shall meet on that beautiful shore." When we finally started attending church years later, I heard a couple of those songs but was disappointed not to hear singing like Nat's.

Naturally, the theme songs to early TV shows and cartoons still dart unannounced into my brain like comets from time to time. Like Roy Rogers' sign-off song, "Happy Trails." Those hypnotic hoofbeats will come out of nowhere, and the melody rides right in. Likewise, the theme song melodies from *The Mickey Mouse Club, The Flintstones, Woody Woodpecker,* or *The Adams Family* (snap, snap). But all of them must bow to the theme song of all time from (what else?) *The Andy Griffith Show,* "The Fishin Hole" song. (You're thinking it now, aren't you. Go ahead. Whistle it.)

It wasn't long, though, until I was into much cooler music than Mom's. I'm talking about sophisticated classics like "Tutti-Frutti," "Bee-Bop-A-Lula," and from the Chipmunks' smash hit version of "Witchdoctor," that most timeless of all choruses: "OOH-EE-OOH-AH-AH-TING-TANG-WALLA-WALLA-BING-BANG." (Talk about a girl magnet. Speak that phrase and they came running.)

That was cool and all, but then it happened. The British invasion. The Fab Four appeared on the *Ed Sullivan Show,* Sunday night, February 9, 1964, and it rocked my world. I turned 12 that summer. Almost every song the Beatles sang was like a theme song for the show that was going on inside me for the next ten years. (The show and the beat still goes on.) "She Loves You," "I Saw Her Standing There," "I Want to Hold Your Hand," "Please, Please Me," "Twist and Shout," "Love Me Do," "And I Love Her," "Help," "I'm Down," "Yesterday," "Nowhere Man," "All You Need Is Love," "Got to Get You into My Life," "The Long and Winding Road."

It was not only a long and winding road; it was a revolution and a revelation. Music became the search engine of a generation and eventually my own divining rod and career.

Somewhere in the middle of those teen years I heard a melody. The circumstance is hazy in my mind but I remember walking past a classroom door. Someone was playing a piano, very slow and tentative, like they were practicing and unsure of the notes. I slowed down to listen. The same phrase played over three or four times. It was so beautiful, sad, and haunting. I peeked into the room, but no one was there. A door to the outside stood open so whoever it was must have just left. I went on and didn't think much of it, but I could not get those notes out of my head. Sometime later I picked them out on a piano somewhere—E E♭ E E♭ E B D C A. Someone standing nearby told me it was a piece called "Für Elise" by Beethoven.

"You mean, Beethoven, of the Beatles' 'Roll Over Beethoven'?"

One and the same.

I never did take piano lessons (one of the major regrets of my life). A few years later, I took up the guitar instead. But to this day, whenever I walk by a piano, those notes are the first thing I'm tempted to play (OK. They are about the only thing I can play on piano.)

During those teen years, my family began to attend church. I'm not sure why, but we did. Amid the noise, insecurity, and hormonal distraction (or attraction) of adolescence, God and things spiritual began to get some of my attention, like the repeated gentleness and beauty of "Für Elise." And some months later, I believed, and was baptized on Easter Sunday. I was fifteen.

Sometime the next year, I was invited to a Baptist youth retreat in New Mexico. So, I went. The two song leaders, the Deitz twins (the very talented Simon & Garfunkel of our high school), had heard that I could carry a tune. So, they asked me to sing a song with them for one of the evening meetings. I was flattered and nervous.

"What song?" I asked.

"Amazing Grace," came the answer. "You sing the melody and we'll sing the harmonies."

I said, "OK. Teach it to me."

They were dumbfounded. "You don't know 'Amazing Grace'?" Apparently, they had never met anyone who didn't know "Amazing Grace."

"Sing a little. Maybe I've heard it," I said. I had been going to church for over a year, but in the back row where I sat with the other teenagers, I may have been otherwise occupied when that song came around.

"You really don't know it?" one of them asked again. I thought I detected a slight concern for my spiritual well-being.

What I didn't know at the time was this: The hymn "Amazing Grace" is to the church what "Yesterday" is to the Beatles—the hit ballad of all time. And for good reason. Both songs so perfectly distill a central experience and longing in the human spirit that whenever they are sung, people tune in and turn toward the sound like flowers to the sun. Even so-called unbelievers cannot resist the sheer power, truth, and beauty.

So, they sang the first verse:

> Amazing grace, how sweet the sound
> That saved a wretch like me
> I once was lost, but now I'm found
> Was blind but now I see
>
> Composed by John Newton, circa 1770 (public domain)

I remember thinking, "What a great song." It was so easy to remember. Every word and every note was exactly as it should be. In sound and symmetry and content, it fit perfectly inside me. (Whenever I've taken long drives with large groups, one of the games we play to pass the time is List Perfect Songs, and that usually includes singing as much as we can remember. Both "Amazing Grace" and "Yesterday" always make the list.)

I sang it back to them. They harmonized, and we sang it together in the meeting. I had found an anthem for life and the twin Baptists were more relaxed about my eternal security.

A YEAR OR SO AFTER THAT, Sarah Saucier, the daughter of my Sunday school teacher, loaned me her guitar to begin learning how to play. A buddy of mine at church, Steve Main, taught me my first chords, and with a lot of help from James Taylor, Bob Dylan, and Jim Croce records, I learned enough to join a band in college. I spent the decade of the '70s studying literature, playing music, growing my hair, wearing bell-bottom jeans, and putting off growing up.

The last two decades, I have spent pursuing a music career and cutting my hair shorter and shorter. I have written hundreds of songs, performed hundreds of concerts, and traveled hundreds of thousands of miles through dozens of countries. I am amazed at two things. First, the global presence and endless varieties of music in every culture. (The staples of our planet appear to be air, water, beans, rice, potatoes, hamburgers, and music.) And second, the world never runs out of new songs. This is true everywhere, but especially where I live, in Nashville, Tennessee. (Around here, when an officer pulls you over for speeding, he always asks, "May I see your license, registration, musical instrument, and I'll need to hear your latest song.") What is the drive in us as a species that continually pours out into melody, rhythm, and song?

In August of 1988, this struck me again. At a family reunion on my mother's side, I was flipping through a scrapbook of the history of her relatives. I ran across this song scribbled on a yellowed piece of paper.

Now tell me, darling
If you will be
Forever faithful, fond and true
And think of the love
I bear for thee
The promises I have made you

And when we join
Each heart and hand
To battle with life's bitter woes
Together we will firmly stand
And share the trouble as it goes

Author J.G. Barnes or unknown, 1892 (public domain)

It was signed, "a compliment of your true friend, J.G. Barnes to Lina Balleu 1892." John Grant Barnes was my great, great uncle. He later married Lina.

I was told that J. G. wrote it as a song and marriage proposal. If he borrowed it from a book somewhere for his own romantic purposes, I haven't been able to find it anywhere. Whatever the case, it's beautiful and a lot more substantial than most love songs and greeting card messages composed a century later.

Driving away from the reunion, I began to put a melody to it, driven by a similar spark that prompted my relative to compose it. (With a few contractions, pick-up notes, and cramming in a syllable here and there, it can be sung to the tune of "Amazing Grace." But it deserves its own melody.) Both John Grant and Lina died many years ago. I couldn't help but feel a new connection with them as I tried different melodies on those beautiful words to find one that would suit it best.

MUSIC IS AN ACT OF REACHING. It is a note in a bottle set adrift on the airwaves. John's note reached Lina. And it reached me nearly a century later. Beethoven reached me from Vienna, Austria across several centuries with "Für Elise." And the Beatles' musical notes floated all the way out to West Texas from Apple Studio in London. Music is such a universal communication link, an invisible bridge, between the seen and the unseen worlds of the sender and the listener.

It wouldn't surprise me if some of the music of this world plays in heaven and vice versa. OK. Maybe not the theme song to *The Addams Family,* though that conjures up a delightful image, but what about "Für Elise" or Handel's *Messiah* or my lullaby "Sail Away"? Songwriters such as John Lennon and Randy Newman have described the experience of melodies drifting into their heads, discoveries not consciously crafted through an act of creative will. The melody to "Yesterday" came to Paul McCartney in a dream. Is music a Morse code of the spirit realm? A shimmering, sonic aurora borealis where two worlds rub together? What if music is scribbled notes passed between not-so-distant relatives? Between the living and souls living on the other side?

> Teen Angel, can you hear me?
> Teen Angel, can you see me?
> Are you somewhere up above?
> And are you still my own true love?
>
> "Teen Angel" by Dion Di Mucci, Fred Patrick, Murray Singer.© 1959—
> 3 Seas Music Corp & Bronx Soul Music (ASCAP). Used by permission.

Or am I reaching, stretching the metaphor, measure by measure, tap dancing to keep the loneliness at bay? To insulate myself from the existential void? I know what I hope. And I am not dancing or singing alone.

Whales sing. Birds whistle and chirp and wail. Wolves and coyotes howl. Crickets scratch out a rhythmic aphrodisiac of insect amour. Even waves crescendo and crash. People the world over hammer out rhythms of passion on clay pots, hollow logs, and drums; on ivory keys and the very ground itself, with sticks and bones and hands and feet. There is a rhythm and pulse to the world. A symphonic resonance. This is not a silent planet. "The mountains and hills will burst into song before you, and all the trees of the field will clap their hands," the prophet Isaiah wrote (Isaiah 55:12 NIV).

A LONG TIME AGO, out of the silence on a hillside in Israel, a shepherd boy named David played and sang songs into the night air. Songs of awe and longing and curiosity. (His greatest hits are in a collection called the Psalms. What a great publishing deal. He has sold more than the Beatles!) David certainly wrote with the assumption that heaven was listening. He was forever singing a new song to the Lord. And he believed heaven, or even God, sang back to him. "He [God] put a new song in my mouth" (Psalm 40:3 NIV).

NOT NEARLY SO LONG AGO, when Willow Grace was about 16 months old, and Kellie was still carrying Wyatt inside her, we drove by a park near our home. It was August or September. The sounds of a symphony came through the open car window. Willow's eyes and mouth grew into big circles. "Oh!" she said in her emotion of first choice—curious delight. We parked, walked over to join the crowd scattered on the grass, and enjoyed a concert under the stars.

Near the end of the performance, the conductor invited the audience to come forward to an open area directly in front of the orchestra. To dance. To a waltz by Johann Strauss. The music of my childhood filled the night. I looked at Kellie. She laughed and said, "It's all right. Go dance with your daughter." So Willow and I waltzed in circles under the moon and stars. And the light that the moon shone down on me shown down on the ones I love. It felt like all of heaven was looking on, listening in, and envious (if envy were possible in heaven). I could have danced all night. And maybe in heaven they did. After all,

> When we've been there ten thousand years
> Bright shining as the sun
> We've no less days to sing God's praise
> Than when we've first begun.
> Composed by John Newton circa 1770 (public domain)

# 6

# Like a Cookie in the Pocket of Heaven

*It's lovely to live on a raft. We had the sky, up
there, all speckled with stars, and we used to
lay on our backs and look up at them, and dis-
cuss about whether they was made, or only just
happened—Jim, he allowed they was made,
but I allowed they happened.*

MARK TWAIN
*Huckleberry Finn*

SOME YEARS AGO, ON A TRIP home through the Dallas/
Fort Worth airport, I bought a Sunday paper and did my
usual—read the funny pages first. On this particular day, Providence (or some wry life force in printer's ink that loves irony)
must have been the editor in charge, because two of my
favorite cartoons, *Ziggy* and *Bloom County*, were positioned

directly across the page from each other. Both depicted exactly the same activity, but from totally different perspectives.

Picture this: On the top left page, Ziggy is out on a hillside with his dog, Fuzz, under a clear, probably summer night sky (judging by his clothing). They are seated, stargazing. In the first four frames, there are no words. The pair simply looks this way and that, their rounded profiles perfectly synchronized. A shooting star darts by. They both turn to see it. Still no words. In the fifth frame, both of them have stood up, and Ziggy is applauding (with all eight of his fat little fingers). Still no words. In the final frame, as he and Fuzz walk off to retire for the night, Ziggy speaks these words toward the starry sky, "Gee, thanks for the evening. It was heavenly."

At the top of the right hand page, the precocious kid genius of *Bloom County*, Oliver Wendell Holmes, is doing the same thing with some obvious differences. He is perched on a short stool on the narrow peak of his rooftop, not on a hillside. He is companionless. It is cold. Snow has piled up on the roof, the hood of his cloak, and his telescope. Evidently, he has been there quite some time. As Oliver observes the night sky through an instrument of science, rather than the naked eye, he documents both the time and his findings in a journal:

First frame: 11:09 P.M. "Cygnus 17 appears normal."

Second frame: 11:23 P.M. "No activity on Jupiter's 3rd moon."

Third frame: 11:40 P.M. "The western sky is looking particularly...empty."

Fourth frame—that entry continues: "...in fact, the entire universe is appearing every bit the meaningless and cold vacuum that it is...Where Truth is relative, God elusive, and Man just an insignificant blob of cosmic spittle." (Spittle is emphatically double underlined.)

Fifth frame: Oliver has removed his spectacles with one hand, rubs one eye with the other and sighs.

Final frame: Oliver, tired and droopy, his hooded head still draped in snow, has tucked the telescope under one arm and called it a night. His last journal entry of the day reads: 11:51 P.M. "Retreats to go listen to a few old Reagan speeches for dramatic renewal of purpose."

My first reaction was exactly what the funny pages intend to evoke. I laughed. Out loud. But this time, it was laughter mixed with amazement.

Beyond the political snipe at Ronald Reagan, both characters view the same universe but arrive at completely opposing conclusions. One sees it full and intentional and assumes a "Someone" behind that intent. The other one sees it empty and without meaning, and its creator, if there is one, inscrutable and undetectable. Why? Is it because one, Ziggy, is simple-minded? Or limited in his analytical capacities to properly ascertain reality from whimsy? And the other, Oliver Wendell, is rational, objective, and able to deduce reality from the evidence verifiable through the only modern, reliable, and credible means—science?

My mind started whirring at the crucial, deep layers of life, both modern and ancient, sketched by two cartoonists in the "funny" pages. How do we know reality? What gives reality meaning? Does it depend on the lens we look through? What makes one person see a half moon hanging in an evening sky and think it looks like a cookie in the pocket of heaven, and another regard the moon as shrapnel from a big bang and nothing else? Where do we get our worldviews? Our identity? Are we "blobs of cosmic spittle"? If so, who spat us out? (We are each a fairly complex organism to be nothing more than what Texans call a "hocker" or a "loogey.") What shapes our belief systems? And how does what we believe affect us? Ziggy seemed genuinely delighted and grateful. Holmes' findings weighed him down and left a vacuum inside him as big as outer space.

Having read *Bloom County* many times before, it was no stretch to conclude that Berkeley Breathed, its creator, was actually making the same point as Tom Wilson, the Zeus of *Ziggy*. Tom, in a Ziggy suit, headed straight for his understated point. Berkeley, I am surmising, beat a longer path to the same place but by means of extreme indirection. He seemed to take the modern line of thinking and extend it logically into a compass heading pointing to existential emptiness. But in so doing, he begged the question in every reader—what every person on the planet must face: Is there more to this time and space science project than meets the eye? Ziggy's answer is applause. Oliver could only sigh.

(When asked about heaven or a life beyond this world, the aging Frank Lloyd Wright said he couldn't imagine anything more beautiful than the natural world. Didn't Mr. Wright design some things not found in nature? He had a large, active imagination. If there is an Architect of heaven and earth, He must be pretty secure to design a Frank Lloyd Wright and give him the freedom to think so small.)

ONCE AGAIN, I WANT YOU to know that I know that this funny page exegesis does not address *why* as much as *what* I think about the nature of things. I suppose I more than tipped my hand toward Ziggy in the first chapter with all that ice cream dream business. But I am simply attempting to describe the character of the universe based on my own observations and experience of it—that and the compelling conclusions of a few others like Ziggy and Oliver Wendell.

These two are not the first to express such divergent views of the creation. From ancient times to the present, people have lined up all down the line from the extreme existential materialists, the what-you-see-hear-touch-taste-smell-measure-and-weigh-is-all-you-get crowd, to the radical nihilists of the nothing-you-see-hear-touch-taste-smell-measure-and-weigh-feel-or-even-imagine-is-real gang. Which group do you think throws a better party? The hedonist, corporate climbers babbling on cell phones or the hedonist, Nietzsche disciples babbling in padded cells? (DON'T drink their punch.) Can you picture their T-shirts?

## ONLY MATTER MATTERS

100% Cotton—Don't be caught dead without one!
Only $29.99 while matter lasts

And on the other side:

## NOTHING REALLY MATTERS

100% Surreal—Don't be caught merely existing without one.
Only $29.99 while the bad dream lasts
(Free Prozac with every purchase.)

It seems the condition of the observer has a lot to do with what is seen. By that I mean: Can the level of pain or pleasure and a belief system combine to cloud or color the lens? (Or can a certain combination of pain, pleasure, and belief system clear the lens enough to actually see a reality substantial enough to be authentic?) What causes Ziggy to agree with the shepherd-king, David, that the heavens declare the glory of God's handiwork (Psalm 19:1)? What pushes Oliver Wendell toward Sartre, Camus, and Sagan who considered the universe neither hostile, nor friendly, but merely indifferent and God not just elusive but absent?

One might assume that a life with fewer traumas might lean a person toward a Ziggy view. And a lot of bad bumps in the road could swing a person toward the more desolate viewpoint expressed by Oliver. However, the opposite can and does happen. I have met many people who, having experienced a fairly trauma-free and rich ride, have quite a dark outlook on life. And I know others who have encountered horrific tragedies who appear remarkably alive to the wonder and fullness of the universe.

One such passionate observer was the Apostle Paul. He was beaten, stoned, shipwrecked, and imprisoned, yet still viewed the creation as an obvious revelation of God and what He is like. He also had a theory about why some can't see it. In fact, he was unabashedly intolerant (forgive him, it was a long time ago and he didn't know any better) of those who saw it but "suppressed the truth" about what their eyes saw. One of his letters reads:

> That which is known about God is evident in them [*those who suppress the truth*]; for God made it evident to them. For since the creation of the world His invisible attributes, His eternal power and divine nature, have been clearly seen, being understood through what has been made, so that they are without excuse. For even though they knew God, they did not honor Him as God or give thanks, but they became futile in their speculations, and their foolish hearts were darkened. Professing to be wise, they became fools (Romans 1:19-21 NASB).

Ouch. Those are strong (some will say strident) statements from a guy who never even had a telescope or the benefit of an "enlightened" modern mind with which to view the cosmos.

Paul seems to think that the crux of this disagreement is *not* a level of hardship or ease of lifestyle but a result of an altered belief system. The clouded lens, what he calls a "darkened heart," results from not acknowledging (as well as believing, honoring, and thanking) God.

I don't doubt that Oliver (as an unwilling spokesgenius and PR kid for the other side of the argument) might counter that

Paul suffered from a darkened mind, *because* he refused to acknowledge the reasonableness of an alternate, Godless theory of the cosmos based on the sheer quantifiable data gathered from the material world. Or, if he chose to meet Paul's adamant stance with the force of current lingo, he might simply write him off by using the old line, "Religion is for weak-minded people."

And then Blaise Pascal, no mental slouch himself, would weigh in with, "S'il vous plaît, gentlemen. The heart experiences God, not the reason."[1]

In the next frame Pascal's diminutive countryman, Napoleon, would counter thrust, "There is no place in a fanatic's head where reason can enter."[2]

Into the following frame a disheveled Nietzsche would wander through and interject, "But even rational thought is interpretation according to a scheme which we cannot escape."[3]

To which Ziggy, in the final frame, might say, "Gee, Friedrich, would you like to stop pacing and lie down while I get you a nice, cool bowl of ice cream?"

MEANWHILE, THE BREACH WIDENS between the heart-ites and the head-ites, and the name-calling and debate still rages around us, and the ink isn't even dry on the first page of the new millennium. Both sides of this not-so-comic strip beg questions even closer to home. Who are *we* in this drama and what part do we play? Cosmic spittle? Useful only to buff the shoes of some cavalier Zeus? Are we kings of the jungle or noble savages in suits? In brains, we're top of the food chain. In cruelty and carnage, bottom of the barrel. Are we animals with retirement plans? The crowning culmination of a mysterious determination inherent in primordial ooze? Are we merely complex co-ops of dust and water driven by electrochemical sparks? Or are we more than the sum of all our parts?

# 7

# Something New
# Under the Sun

*I cannot see my soul but I know 'tis there.*

—EMILY DICKINSON

I ONCE LIVED FOR TWO YEARS on eighteen acres out in the country. Someone boarded several cows in the pasture, and of the many lessons I could have learned from them, this is the only one that stuck.

One hot summer afternoon, I saw a cow standing in the creek. Even a creature as dumb as a cow (perhaps "ignorant as a cow" is kinder or at least more accurate) knows that shade and water are preferable to a treeless, sun-baked pasture. The cow, facing downstream in about fifteen inches of current, contributed to the flow by urinating upstream while drinking from its own country cocktail. The bored, bovine eyes registered absolutely no awareness of the rancid recycling taking place. I actually took two life lessons from this parable: one, never vote for anyone who would place a landfill near a drinking water source, and two, I am at least smarter than a cow.

This heightened awareness is compelling yet, unfortunately, not conclusive evidence that we humans are greater than the sum of our parts. For whenever I see some of my fellow Earthlings dumping toxic fumes into the air or destroying the forests that replenish the air we breath, I recall that vision and have to conclude that at least some of us, some of the time, are no smarter than cows.

Be that as it may, just because we are smart enough to urinate downstream from our drinking source, does that shed any light on who we are in the big scheme of things?

WELL INTO MY ADULT YEARS, an event from early school days resurfaced in my memory after being long submerged. It runs so deep and strong, and had been following below my little vessel all along like some sort of benevolent guardian whale.

Most school days and classes are such a blur of smudges in the mind. But not this day. Not this class. I was in the eighth grade. Mrs. Thompson's general science class. She was tall, calm, and kind. I was skinny, fidgety, and shy. We were beginning a new chapter. I can still see the title on the left-hand page of the open book: "The Human Species." I suppose that day is so indelible for many reasons but mainly because Mrs. Thompson spent the entire class on the first sentence of the chapter. It contained only three words: You are unique.

I understood that on one level. I was the skinniest kid in school. In the seventh grade, I weighed seventy pounds. In the eighth, I weighed eighty. While almost everyone else was growing up and out, I put on only ten pounds a year through high school and graduated at a whopping one hundred and twenty-three pounds. In junior high, guys used to wrap their hands around my skinny wrists to see how far they could overlap their fingers. I used to sit and wonder why I was made this way. I remember thinking, "I could break my own arms, if I only had the strength."

So I knew I was unique. But Mrs. Thompson had a whole new slant. She often illustrated what she taught in creative ways. For instance, I remember she made us aware of the constant pull of gravity by challenging us to hold one arm out in the aisle as long as we could. No sweat, we all thought, especially the guys. Mrs. Thompson went on teaching to a room full of kids with arms stuck out in the air like a flock of geese signaling a group right turn. After only a few minutes, some groaning began, from the girls first, and despite our efforts, arms began to sag toward the linoleum. Soon, over-dramatic agonies filled the room. We were amazed that we couldn't command our own arms to obey. No one lasted more than twenty-five minutes. Gravity won and so did Mrs. Thompson.

SHE WON THIS DAY, TOO. I remember her showing us leaves and pictures of snowflakes. She emphasized how no two in the world were exactly alike, and there were billions. We studied our hands and compared them to other hands in the class to see the differences in shape and lines and fingerprints. All the while Mrs. Thompson hammered it home, "There are nearly four billion people in the world and there is not another person just like you. Never has been and never will be." (We have recently passed the six billion mark, and I suspect that every one of the two billion babies born since then are originals.)

OF COURSE, THIS WAS ALL to set up the fascinating world of chromosomes and genes and mitosis and meiosis. But more happened that day, at least in me. I got hooked on biology and for the next five years wanted to be a marine biologist. Even deeper though, something got hooked inside me.

I was not aware of God nor had I given Him much thought during that time. But that day in Mrs. Thompson's class, a seed of truth attached itself to my soul like the burrs in my socks on our Boy Scout hikes. I'm glad this one couldn't be plucked out as easily. Two years passed before I became a Christian, and not long after, a less than scientific source confirmed the same truth when I read another view of how intimately and intricately God had knit me together.

> For You [O God] formed my inward parts; You wove me in my mother's womb. I will give thanks to You, for I am fearfully and wonderfully made; wonderful are Your works, and my soul knows it very well. My frame was not hidden from You, when I was made in secret, and skillfully wrought in the depths of the earth. Your eyes have seen my unformed substance...
>
> (Psalm 139:13-16 NASB).

(That's quite different from regarding someone as a superfluous blob of cosmic spittle.)

Looking back I wondered if Mrs. Thompson had any motives other than scientific and if her kindness and gracious manner arose from a natural love of junior high kids or something more. I wondered if she believed in God.

A few years ago, after singing a few songs in my parents' church in Texas, a woman walked up and introduced herself. It was Mrs. Thompson. We laughed and were amazed that our paths should cross again in such a setting so many years and miles down the river since my eighth-grade school year. She was surprised at what I do for a living, especially that it includes standing up in front of so many people. She remembered me as such a skinny and extremely shy boy.

I seized the chance to tell her that I sometimes refer to her in concerts and seminars, and reminded her of that day in her class so many years ago. She vaguely recalled that part of her yearly lesson plan, but, of course, had no idea how monumental it was to me. We spent only a few minutes together but it was such a remarkable coincidence of staggering odds given the years, 30, times distance, times number of people in Texas, times the number of students Mrs. Thompson taught over her career, factoring in the divergent lives of all those students and each of their family storylines. (Did I mention the weather? Traffic? Or the common cold virus, any one of which could have prevented this meeting from ever happening?) Or then again, maybe it was a divinely choreographed encounter.

In a world where life has become so cheap and human beings so disposable, Mrs. Thompson, and (perhaps totally unbeknownst to him) the writer of the science textbook, planted a seed in me that day. A seed of self-identity, which later sprouted into a profound reality. I am singular. Unrepeatable. I am the only me that will ever be. What value that places on any one of us above a fleeting but unique snowflake can be debated. But if I am only a blob of cosmic spittle, I am at least unique spittle.

Mrs. Thompson never imagined all that happened in me in that fifty-minute class all those years ago. I didn't realize it all at the time either. She was just going through her lesson plan, playing her part. Her "You Are Unique" lesson plan probably didn't get to everybody in that classroom. But it got to me. And it stuck somewhere inside.

There was a season (I believe it's called youth) when I remained conveniently and selectively oblivious to the miracle of every human being, especially those far away or out of sight, the hungry and homeless down the block or in third world countries, or the unborn. But the set-you-free effect of that seed of truth has by degrees made me less able to insulate myself from hurting about and caring for those unique miracles in need.

The daily sandpaper of time and a few funerals along the way have stripped away even more of that insulation. Nothing magnifies the huge significance of one individual like death.

But at long last, perhaps the ultimate awakening has occurred. I now have two mitosis/meiosis miracles in my home. Emmaline Willow Grace and William Van Wyatt. A moment after Willow was born, I began to plant the same truth in her. I cued one of my songs, "Kumquat May," in a tape deck to begin at the chorus—"You are the best thing under the sun/No one like you since time was begun."

It was her first lesson in "You Are Unique." I know old King Solomon said there is nothing new under the sun, but he never laid eyes on my little ones. I'm sure (like most parents) that would change his tune. (The first song Wyatt heard was "Here Comes the Sun" from the Beatles' *Abbey Road* album. I guess you can take the boy out of the '60s but you can't take the '60s out of the boy.)

I HAVE WITNESSED BIRTH and seen death. I have watched God, or Cosmos, if you prefer, continue to play His part by creating children, spitting out one-of-a-kind, unduplicated miracles. A molecular marriage of protoplasm and psyche. A finite machine aware of infinity. An exquisite timepiece with eyes of blue heaven.

Some highly articulate blobs of cosmic spittle insist we are merely upstream on the genetic pecking order from cows. Others have concluded that if you connect all the dots, God is still sketching himself in the shape of Willow, Wyatt, and my nephews and nieces Ryan, Sydney, Kyle, Hailey, Krista, and Lance. Many are convinced that all the little children—red, yellow, black, brown, and white—bring His image into sight. I have decided to side with them, so I keep birthing songs and raising a glass to miracle number six billion and one, and counting. Maybe that's part of playing my part.

Naked arrival
Primordial scream
You're a beautiful Bloom
From the garden of your Grandmother Eve
Made by your Maker
Like a Clock with a soul
And there's a fingerprint of His
Like a tattoo on your chromosomes

Here's to life in the cradle of Eden
Long before the world began
Here's to life from the laughing Creator
Sketching Himself in the shape of man

Back in the mailroom
Way up in the sky
When the Father put a stamp on your soul
There was a tear in His eye
Cause the currents of evil
Threaten your course from the start
But He smiled when He wrote His address
On the back of your heart

Chorus

Come drink the days, taste the Time
So glad you're here and here's to Life
Baby, welcome to the lovely
Baby, welcome to the lovely
Baby, welcome to the lovely ride

# 8

# A Lovely, Dangerous Road

*Welcome to the sacred journey*
*That every mother's child must make*
*A lovely, dangerous road,*
*You better find a hand to hold*

"THE SACRED JOURNEY"
© 1993 Paragon Music Corp./ Skin Horse, Inc.
(ASCAP) by Billy Sprague. Used by permission.

OK. So, LIFE ISN'T ALWAYS SUCH a lovely ride. Can anyone quibble with that, aside from Ziggy and other fictional characters who become extinct (except in syndication) when their creators die but can never really know pain, suffering, grief, despair, and death? As for all non-fiction, flesh-and-blood ticket holders, you hang on and swing between agony and ecstasy until your grip fails and six friends carry your carcass to the countryside and ceremoniously plant you in a field of memories. Nice ride. (Look out for the last turn, it'll kill you.)

But why worry a newborn human with the less than splendid episodes of the journey? Calamities from acne to cancer, violence both natural and man-made, and unanswerables of mind-numbing, heart-rending proportions await the unsuspecting babe who generates such joy and affection. Or maybe we are born suspicious. Maybe we doubt the worthiness of the gift of life right from the first gulp of air. And that's why we begin with a cry.

Is all the joy worth all the sorrow and suffering? It depends on who you ask and when you ask them. Solomon seemed pretty fired up about life in the amorous musings of Song of Songs when all the hormones of youthful vigor were coursing through him and his sights were set on some young lovely whose delectable attributes were ripe for the picking. But hundreds of wives and concubines later, the old preacher who wrote Ecclesiastes (also attributed to Solomon, the wisest man who ever lived) concluded upon looking back, "all is meaningless" (Ecclesiastes 1:2). But then he reversed himself and seemed just as certain that God designed "an appointed time for everything under heaven" (Ecclesiastes 3:1). You may know the list from the old Byrds' song, "Turn, Turn, Turn." "A time to be born. A time to die." A time for Planting—Harvesting. Killing—Healing. Destruction—Construction. Weeping—Laughing. Mourning—Dancing. Stone throwing—Stone gathering. Embracing—Refraining. Searching—Losing. Keeping—Discarding. Tearing—Mending. Silence—Words. Love—Hate. War and Peace.

So, which is it, preacher? Meaningless? Or designed with Divine intent and, therefore, full of meaning? Solomon seems extremely conflicted on this. (But I am not the wisest man who ever lived.)

Is life a "tale told by an idiot, full of sound and fury, signifying nothing," as Macbeth concluded? Do we row gently,

gently, gently down the stream, in a denial-driven psychosis singing "merrily, merrily life is but a dream," as one songwriter suggested? Or do we refuse to "go gentle into that good night" and instead "rage, rage against the dying of the light," as Dylan Thomas urged his dying father. (Certainly the passion of the poem is as much a cry of the deep measure of the poet's love for his father as it is a protest against the outrageous and stubborn reality of death.) Will such a dramatic outburst add one cubit or dash of meaning to our days? Or bring any clarity or resolution to the final equation: Life + Time = Dead and Gone? (Or is that the final equation?)

Is this a sacred journey or just a hazardous field trip with an unavoidable destination, the grave? Even without a God factor, not everyone subscribes to the uniqueness and intrinsic value of every person. And without that, any sense of holiness (or even the most noble secular social contract) evaporates like morning mist, and anything goes. Look at the unspeakable horrors we inflicted on each other in the last century alone. And yet millions continue to cling to the notion that embodied in each and every individual is a holy chalice containing the essence or spirit that animates us beyond the sheer mechanics of biology and makes us more than the sum of our dissectable parts.

Isn't that really why thousands of people stream past the Mona Lisa every day? Isn't that why the whole wired-to-CNN world tunes in to watch the rescue effort when a child falls down a well in China? Isn't that why one of my younger brothers, Brad, received the highest Boy Scout award for rescuing a lady from her sinking car? Isn't that why he jumped into the water at all? Isn't that why murder is the most grievous, heinous offense? Isn't that why abortion is such a hot button and divisive issue? Isn't that why the name Anne Frank shines like an eternal flame against the dark chapter of organized evil that miscalculated the holy power of good?

*Anne, I read your book on my first trip to Amsterdam in July of 1986. After touring your hiding place, I bought your diary at the bookstore downstairs and walked to a small outdoor café around the corner. I read the whole thing sitting there drinking some strong, frank Dutch coffee. The bells in a nearby tower rang just as you described, and I began to see the world through your eyes. I kept my sunglasses on to hide my tears.*

*I have traveled to Amsterdam three times and visited your hiding place on every trip. The second and third times, I lingered longer. I found myself touching the doorknobs and water faucets where your hands must have landed many times and whispering, "We remember you, Anne. We remember."*

*Years later, I still remember you. I took up painting a few years ago and, when I decided to attempt a portrait, yours was the first face I painted. It is my own personal Mona Lisa and hangs on my studio wall. More recently, I co-wrote a song with you in mind. The third verse is all yours. I hope you like it.*

> Anne had a dream to be a writer
> She put it all down in her diary
> Here's to the friends who tried to hide her
> From the Great Atrocity
> O, it took her life but not her dream
>
> Love is brave—at facing the night
> Believing in the daylight
> Love will stay—strong in the heart of the heartache
> Love is brave

"Love is Brave" © 1999 Careers-BMG Music Publishing, Inc. (BMI)
Skin Horse, Inc. (ASCAP) Sara Hart/Billy Sprague (used by permission)

*You were very brave, Anne.*

*In one of your sad moments, you wrote, "The world will go on without me." It has, like it will without any of us, but it is brighter because of you. You also wrote, "I want to go on living even after my death." You have. Remember wondering if you would ever write anything really great? Well, you did. Your diary is a wonderful book. An important book. You've sold millions of copies around the world. You still help us be brave. You helped me be brave through a long night of grief. You longed to be heard, Anne. You still are. And no one will ever silence you.*

In fact, Anne Frank is compelling evidence for me that good is stronger than evil. Certainly good will take a beating along the way, because life is not just a lovely road. It's dangerous. Hazardous. And yet, people, millions of them, still believe in the sanctity, the holiness, the ordained ordering of life and even death. Not only did a depressed, wise old king who experienced every luxury this world can offer believe this, but the marvel is, those who have faced the hazards head-on believe it. I saw this no clearer than on a trip to Poland in July of 1990.

PICTURE A HUGE, WHITE CIRCUS TENT pitched next to a small wheatfield set amid rolling, forested hills much like those of middle Tennessee. Under and spilling out around the tent are three to four thousand men, women, and children, mostly Poles, many Czechs, even a few Russians. After a local translates the song lyric from English to Polish, they obediently mimic an American singer attempting to teach them the response part of a song in English with a British accent. And picture it working.

"I can believe," I sing.

"In a hazardous world" (pronounced "ha-za-dus wuld"), they respond, in their most charming Slavic/British accent.

"I'm down on my knees,"

"In a ha-za-dus wuld," comes back from the crowd.

"With every breath that I breathe,"

"In a ha-za-dus wuld," they sing.

"I can believe."

As I remember this rare moment and that whole day of my trip to Poland and Eastern Europe, it seemed even then like I was watching it from a corner in the top of the tent or from treetop level all day long.

It was Saturday, the sixth day in a weeklong series of evangelistic meetings in southern Poland. In the morning, our small group of Americans set out in two cars to visit Auschwitz death camp. Anne Frank's mother, Edith, died there. Her father, Otto, survived Auschwitz and was liberated by the Russians in April 1945. Anne and her sister, Margo, spent three months there before being shipped to Bergen-Belsen camp in Germany where they died of typhus in March of 1945, just weeks before the war ended in May.

Our mood grew more somber as we approached the compound. Such a place makes words irreverent. I had read of the horrors and seen some of the black-and-white WWII film footage. But to walk into the scene of sheer evil defies description. The double row of barbed, electrified fences. The killing wall, pockmarked by bullets. The hanging posts. The gas chambers and human ovens. All these enforce a silent lament for those who suffered there in the diabolical harvest of millions of lives. In some cells, prisoners had scratched names or dates into the walls. I ran my fingers over some of the markings, I suppose in a futile attempt to make contact with some living souls who had made an effort to be remembered. I began to whisper, "We remember, We remember you," through peep holes in the cell doors and into the hollow gas chambers. The memories are indelible in me still.

We stayed only a few hours, saw a brief film and then headed back, quiet and more certain than ever about the reality of this hazardous world.

LATER, IN THE MIDDAY SESSION, some of us learned folk dances in the dirt road by the wheatfield as the worship band played a Jewish-sounding song. Old peasant women, survivors of many hazards, watched us. How odd we must have appeared to them. The speaker, a German who also toured

Auschwitz that morning with us, set aside his planned message and spoke through tears of shame that his countrymen could commit such atrocities. He went on to speak so passionately of man's desperate need for a change of heart by reconnecting with God.

Anne could not have agreed more.

> There is a great urge and rage in people to destroy, to kill, to murder, and until all mankind, without exception, undergoes a great change, wars will be waged. (Wednesday, May 3, 1944)

> I see the world gradually being turned into a wilderness, I hear the ever-approaching thunder, which will destroy us too, I can feel the sufferings of millions and yet, if I look up into the heavens, I think that it will all come right, that this cruelty too will end, and that peace and tranquility will return. (Saturday, July 15, 1944)

From *The Diary of Anne Frank: The Critical Edition* by Anne Frank, copyright ©1986 by Anne Frank-Fonds, Basle/Switzerland, for all texts of Anne Frank. Used by permission of Doubleday, a division of Random House, Inc.

Three weeks after she wrote that, the Germans raided the secret annex, on Friday, August 4, and took Anne and the others away.

IN THE LATE AFTERNOON MEETING, I stood on the platform looking at the many pleasant, eager, and weary faces, most of them believers in spite of a hazardous world...all of them living in countries emerging from years of hardship under communist governments. These were true believers. Though the Berlin wall was down and new freedoms were at hand, they did not believe in democracy as the light of the world. Their light came from a different source. They knew that democracy brings certain freedoms. But it cannot make them free. They had faced the night and believed in and made it to the daylight of a new era. And now they stood shoulder to shoulder bathed in golden light...like the field of wheat beside the big white tent.

We looked at each other, on this strange, remarkable day, and finished the chorus:

> "There are no guarantees..."
> "In a ha-za-dus wuld."
> "Makes no difference to me..."
> "In a ha-za-dus wuld."
> "God sent His own Son to bleed..."
> "In a ha-za-dus wuld."
> "I can believe."

And they sang like true believers.

# 9

# Holding the Intangible

*I believe in harbors at the end.*

THOMAS WOLFE

WE ARE THE ONLY SPECIES THAT believes. I may wax poetic and say that the seed beneath the snow believes in the spring or my cat or dog believes it is part of the family, but those are only expressions. By "believing," I do not mean theorizing and then testing via the scientific method (although we are the only species that does that, too—OK, here comes the letter from the anthropoidologist making the case for chimps). And believing is not merely assuming an unseen reality completely without evidence.

Believing involves an awareness, a hunch. About eternity. That spark in the human psyche may be the strongest evidence of a reality beyond the material universe. This longing begs the question, "Is there more to the world, and you and me, than meets the eye?"

Certainly, believing doesn't make a thing so. LSD can convince some people they can fly. Sadly, a few have made sincere attempts and forfeited their lives for that belief. But disbelieving doesn't make it unso. For centuries we did not believe that the earth revolved around the sun.

What intrigues me is not only what is believed (what some people believe can be quite amazing), but the drive or need in us to believe in something. That seems to me to set us apart, like praying and pride, from all the other creatures. Everybody believes something. And believing shapes our lives dramatically.

For instance, I once met a lady on a return trip from Europe. We were seated near each other on a jumbo jet, and about halfway into the trip, we stood in the aisle to stretch our legs and chatted. She was returning to Florida. I asked her where she had visited in Europe. That's all it took to prime the pump. For the next half-hour she described to me (and a half-dozen or so captive passengers within earshot) the conference she had attended in Holland. She was animated and a little loud. She had paid thousands of dollars to attend a meeting of world-renowned psychics who, for a healthy fee, guided the attendees through a discovery process about their past lives. Much of her excitement came from the clarity she had gained about her life, personality and déjà vu experiences.

The most remarkable part of her story was who she claimed to have been. Of her four or five previous, possible identities (the experts had emphasized "possible"), all were famous people. There was no obscure medieval peasant/servant girl or brothel slave or sweatshop seamstress dying of consumption in her psychic lineage. And no non-white, non-Anglo-Saxons either. She had "possibly" been one of King Henry VIII's wives. She had "possibly" been Marie Antoinette. And there were strong "indicators," as the clinicians called them, that she may have been Joan of Arc. At this point, several passengers glanced incredulously at each other and returned to their novels or pillows. I could not disconnect without extreme rudeness, and besides, I was fascinated.

The woman borrowed quite an ennobling buoyancy from the potentiality of this psychic information. She spoke with an air of epic tragedy like someone who had drunk directly from the Holy Grail of revelation. (I think some bourbon was involved as well.)

She finally asked me the highlight of my trip. I began to tell her about my visit to Anne Frank's hiding place. At the mention of Anne's name, the woman's eyes widened and, you guessed it, she had been Anne Frank. Or at least the well-paid psychic counselor had pointed to strong "indicators" that she certainly had been someone very close to Anne, who also died in a concentration camp, or actually "might" have been Anne Frank.

In my stunned silence I did some quick timeline calculations. This lady appeared to be between 35 and 40 or so in age. This was 1986. That would make her birth date just after WWII. Anne died in March of 1945. So that would work. Anne's shining soul or psyche might "possibly" have left her body in Bergen-Belsen death camp, lingered wherever souls in transit linger, traveled (or was transferred by the Psyche Conductor) to south Florida (presuming that to be her birth place) where a young couple were making love, entered the womb via fertilization (or whenever that occurs) to emerge into the world, again, becoming her current incarnation, a well-dressed, white, Jewish (obviously not Orthodox), non-famous female desperately panning for nuggets of significance from her own stream of consciousness.

I resisted the temptation to say, "May I speak to Anne now?"

After all, who am I to throw cold water on a sincere search for meaning? I have panned for nuggets from my own river of dreams. As Viktor Frankl (a concentration camp survivor himself) said in *Man's Search for Meaning*, as a species we are inveterate meaning mongers. We are all looking for a sense of destiny and identity. We are all asking the same questions: Who am I? Why am I here? Where did I come from? Am I going anywhere after this journey? What is the meaning of life? (And in the meantime, where can you get a really thick milkshake?)

Instead, I looked at her and calmly asked what I really wanted to know, "Do you really believe all this?" She only said that parts of it helped explain some things about her life and personality.

And then she put me on the spot. Without any defensive tone, but still loud enough for the surrounding passengers to hear, she asked, "What do you believe?" She sincerely wanted to know.

The scene felt immediately like an old brokerage commercial where one person asks another on a crowded subway platform, "What does your broker say?" The other person responds, "My broker is So and So and he says..." at which point all activity and talking stops and everyone leans in to hear his answer.

I remember making it as simple as I could. I told her I believe the old, old story. That God created the world. Made us to resemble Him in certain ways. We each have a one-of-a-kind eternal spirit. We are estranged from God and each other because of rebellion, or sin, to use the old word. God became one of us, Jesus, in order to reconnect us with Himself. He sacrificed His one human life to do that and then came to life again to prove who He was and that death is not the end. We live one life, die, our bodies return to the dust and our spirits go to God. After death there is a judgment based on whether we believe in Him. I told her I believe what the eyewitnesses said, that before He rose into the sky, Jesus told them He would prepare a place for us called heaven where there will be no more tears, pain, evil, confusion, or goodbyes. Someday He will return to take all believers there, and we will have new death-proof bodies and will eat and drink and celebrate at an amazing reunion. And the whole motivation for all of this is God's love. (I didn't mention the ice cream dream, though I'm sure she would have enjoyed that. Besides, at the time I don't think its significance had dawned on me.)

When I finished, my orthodox spiel felt a little under-whelming compared to her star-studded belief system, except for the part about Jesus coming to life again. I always thought there could be nothing more impressive than that.

I braced myself for a discussion of the tolerance of various beliefs and the sincerity of the believers of other world religions, or a debate about whether Jesus actually rose from the dead and how do we really know what is true and who really has the whole truth, etc., but she was thoughtfully quiet. I remember her saying something like, "A place like that would be nice." I agreed.

We talked a little more about life and what we did for a living. We exchanged business cards and took our seats. She returned to her life in Florida and I went back to mine in Tennessee. We actually exchanged a letter or two (this was before e-mail). I sent her some music and the river that brought us together carried us apart. I wonder where else her search has taken her.

SHE WAS NOT THE ONLY SEARCHER driven by a need to believe that I ran into on that trip. I met a three-thousand-year-old mummy in the British Museum in London. As I admired his gold jewelry, a professor leading a group of students filed in next to me. For the next twenty minutes, I audited the class as the learned Egyptologist explained the significance of each artifact.

He drew particular attention to a carved stone scarab beetle, which looks like a cross between a ladybug and a dung beetle. It seems every Egyptian of low or high rank was buried with one of these over the heart. The professor recited from memory the prayer that went with the beetle. It was a plea that in the afterlife, when the person was weighed in the balance by the sun god, Osiris, (represented by a man with the head of a hawk), the heart would not be found lacking. The stone beetle was intended to tip the scales in the believer's favor and help gain admittance to paradise.

BACK HOME, AND MANY CENTURIES later, I discovered the Egyptians were not the only ones to put their faith in rocks. Standing at the register at one of my favorite restaurants, I noticed the young cashier had a beautiful stone on her necklace. She seemed to be having a less than pleasant day. Her expression, or lack of it, made me wonder if she had fought with her boyfriend just before her shift or her dog had been run over that morning. I admired the stone and asked her what it was, expecting to hear something like topaz or vermilion quartzite. Instead, she said in a sigh, without moving her jaw, "It's my power stone."

I had heard of that so I asked, "What does it do?"

She touched the stone with one hand while totaling my order with the other and said, "It purges my negative energy and helps keep me clear and balanced."

It didn't seem to be working.

A thought came to me I probably should have resisted but failed. It was a feeble attempt to brighten her day. I said, "Ex-Lax does that for me but it doesn't make good jewelry." In the wrong hands, a tongue is a dangerous thing. She was not amused. I still like to think she laughed later. But I can be dim as granite.

I HAVE A VERY TALL, LARGE-HEARTED friend who carves stone for a living. Many of his works are variations of a sweeping elliptical shape in which the stone pours back through an opening in itself and then curves back around to reach and pour again. They are liquid snapshots of some folded Einstein universe forever chasing its own tail. He has created dozens of them. Some are of smooth soapstone an inch long. Some are larger, translucent alabaster worthy to adorn a table in a fine home or museum. Others glow in exotic highly polished marble several feet tall and are poised upright to revolve on a single steel post. I often wondered what drives him to carve the shape again and again.

In his studio one day, I asked him about this. He opened drawer after drawer to reveal hundreds of them. Even as a boy he began to carve the shape. He is not sure himself what it is. I wonder if it's the tangible, visual metaphor of the object of his search or just the shape of the process of searching?

In either case, he is a believer in something beyond. He believes in God. Admires Jesus. Wrestles with the narrow aspects of Christianity. Thinks reincarnation makes good sense in order for the soul to become wise and at last truly loving. He believes in eternity and carves the infinity shape again and again.

On one occasion he came to listen to me sing and carved something small in his big hands as he listened. I half-expected it to be a variation of "the shape." Afterward he gave it to me. It was a beautiful whorled shell carved out of rose soapstone.

Another time, he attended our Annual Ceremony of the Golden Scoop. Every year at the peak of the ceremony, I descend onto the deck carrying a leather-bound treasure chest to present the golden scoop, to which the attendees respond with the ceremonial "Oohs" and "Aahs." That year, when I opened the chest, the golden scoop had been replaced. He had carved a piece that combined two of my great affections—an ice cream scoop with a whale tail handle. It is one of my great treasures. He is large in spirit and gifts and inspiring to be around, so much so that I and another friend, who is a marvelous sculptor of songs, co-carved a song with "the shape" in mind.

You've heard the stories
And read the message in the pages
You consider crucifixion
Is it a fact or fiction for the ages?
Did He really appear
Like they say that He did?
Does it conquer the fear?
Did He die so that we could live?
You'd like to believe that it's true

O, but you want to hold the intangible
Fashion the darkness into familiar shape
To see with your eyes
To know in your mind
Oh ye of so little faith
Only the heart can hold the intangible

There is a chamber
In the soul of the believer
It holds reason in defiance
And the demanding hand of science may not enter
But let's just suppose
How it would be
To trade all you know
For one ounce of true belief
You'd learn the peace of that place

It seems we all have faith in something. The lady on the plane put her money on the credibility of other human beings to see behind the scrim of the physical world and discern a "possible" cycle of spiritual choreography. The Egyptians placed their bets on a bug and a prayer. The young, cheerless cashier spent her hourly wage and leaned her spiritual and emotional balance on a glimmer of hope in a sparkling crystal. As for my friend, the sculptor, maybe he is a descendant of a scarab beetle carver at a funerary shop in Cairo (or "possibly" was him many lives ago) and perhaps his lineage includes Michelangelo and Rodin.

In Michelangelo's *Madonna and Child* at Notre Dame in Bruges, Belgium, the boy Jesus is seated on Mary's lap. She holds his hand. For the unbeliever (there are no non-believers), it is only a compelling picture, a mythical metaphor in stone of mankind's desire to hold the intangible. But for believers, it depicts the actual contact point where Deity revealed more than its backside to Moses. God placed Himself in our hands. Emmanuel, God with us, as the story goes, got hungry, ate, fished, cried, and walked (on water).

Likewise, Michelangelo's *Pieta* freezes the moment of agony when the intangible, the "image of the invisible God" (Colossians 1:15 NASB), succumbed to death and slipped from His mother's hand and our grasp. Three days later, as the story goes, the intangible reappeared, cooked fish, ate, walked through walls, hung around for a few weeks, and then levi-tated out of reach back into the heavens leaving a few hundred witnesses in a world full of searchers.

To some viewers, like Oliver Wendell from *Bloom County*, my sculptor friend's infinity shape might be a modern version of Rodin's *The Thinker*, forever frozen in the cul-de-sac of reason. I wonder if it isn't his own abstract *Madonna and Child* or *Pieta*, an image of the invisible mystery he may fashion with his hands, but for now, can only hold in his heart, like any of us, by believing.

# 10

# Memos to the Almighty

*I have had prayers answered—most strangely so sometimes—but I think our heavenly Father's loving-kindness has been even more evident in what He has refused me.*

LEWIS CARROLL
From *The Letters of Lewis Carroll*

WE ARE THE ONLY SPECIES THAT PRAYS. I would love to be wrong about this and someday discover that every bird and whale song is a prayer and not just an instinct-driven lure or lament.

The first time I remember praying to God—I mean actually and earnestly talking to the air in the hope that Someone is really there—was on a Boy Scout camping trip. (The one I mentioned in an earlier chapter). After the five-mile hike, and being left for many hours, I am alone on the prairie, waiting for one of the clueless adults to come back and pick me up. After sunset, and after the point where I believe I will die from exposure, starvation, prickly pear apple thorns, coyotes, or rattlesnakes, I begin to complain to God. It is more like a pity party than a prayer. *Why me? I'm too young to die. It'll serve them right for leaving me. God, if You can hear me, help me. Help someone find me.* Someone does. Finally.

I suppose God heard me. I can't say whether He answered my prayer or whether someone simply realized I was long overdue. Maybe God reminded them. Maybe He kept the coyotes and rattlesnakes away. Or maybe I was too skinny and full of self-pity for their taste.

A FEW YEARS LATER...My family begins to attend a church. One Sunday evening at a youth meeting, the leader, Ron, asks me to say an opening prayer. I have never prayed aloud in front of people. I try to sound religious and sincere, fumbling along, borrowing phrases from adult prayers. *Dear God, Thank You for this day and...uh, this place and...uh, this opportunity to meet and...uh, be with us, and...uh, (long pause) in Jesus' name, Amen.* (I sounded like Mr. Stamps, my seventh-grade Texas history teacher. He was so boring we used to pass the time counting how many times he said "and...uh," during the class. His record was fifty-seven.)

I remember feeling embarrassed, inept, exposed as an amateur prayer. Ron's prayers were relaxed and real talk. He spoke to God reverently but naturally, in his everyday tone, not in a from-the-pulpit style. I don't know how God felt about my prayer. Maybe He yawned and counted the "and...uhs." Maybe He was just glad to hear from me at all.

TWO YEARS LATER...early June...Thursday night, during a "night of silence" at church camp, I am sitting on a picnic table under a clear, star-filled sky talking to God. I have not yet seen great evil or suffering, death or despair close up. (My sins involve lying and stealing Coke bottles from open garages.) Over the last year, I have been coming to some sense of my fragile and obscure position in the universe. Any feeling of need for God is recent, mainly because I lost my virginity this spring and for the first time I feel like a sinner, like I have deliberately gone against God's will in a big way. So in simple language, without understanding how it all works, I tell God I believe and ask Him to forgive me and save me through the sacrifice Jesus made and to take me to heaven some day when I die. I cannot describe the overwhelming sense of comfort and the lift in my heart that occurs in the next moments. Through the tears and silence a lightness, a tender nearness, and solitary embrace, come over me like I have never known. I am consoled and know I am forgiven, accepted, and out from under any condemnation from God. It is a calm euphoria.

Even now when I describe that experience, my heart softens and reconnects with a reality no philosopher or psychologist can explain away.

THREE YEARS LATER… One month before graduation, the high school guidance counselor calls me to her office. With great pleasure she informs me I have been granted a full four-year scholarship to any university of my choosing in the state of Texas because of my scoliosis—curvature of the spine—a condition my dad discovered a year earlier when he saw me doing a few shirtless pushups to enhance my hundred-and-ten-pound physique. She explains that a surplus of Texas oil revenue has been set aside to ensure productive lives for potentially physically-challenged citizens. Without my knowledge she applied for me.

Many of my buddies knew by February of our senior year where they will attend college in the fall. I had done more praying about the future than sending out applications, more out of fuzzy-headed procrastination than any deep spiritual reliance on the hand of Providence.

A YEAR LATER... I lie in a hospital bed in Houston the night before surgery. For two years I have prayed to be healed from scoliosis. I remember the place in the Bible where Jesus said, "Whatever you ask of the Father in my name, He will give you." I use His own words like a contractual clause He must live up to. Like a checkmate move on the Almighty. *Dear God, please heal me before morning, in Jesus' name.* Before daylight the nurses come in and wheel me off to the O.R., where a team of specialists cut my back open like a watermelon, fuse seven vertebrae, screw two steel rods into my bones, and stitch me up. I spend the next nine months in a body cast. During the incubation of that unanswered prayer, I learn to play the guitar, scour the New Testament beginning to end, and become good friends with my mother, Oteka, who takes such good care of me.

I see now what Lewis Carroll meant. God refused me this request and answered strangely. That year was a critical turning point of my life. Being marooned (although more briefly than Robinson Crusoe) redirected my life. I had other (and perhaps more serious) ailments to be delivered from than scoliosis, and other prayers that took priority on the Great Physician's chart. Lack of faith. Focus. Life direction. Discipline. I read the Bible daily and practiced the guitar for hours on end. I discovered a personal faith that replaced the one gathered secondhand, and tapped into an undeveloped musical gift that would become my vocation. Where would I be today if God had healed my back that night?

SPRING OF 1979... En route to Fort Worth, Texas, from Austin I write a lullaby called "Dream a Dream." It is a song to sing a child to sleep. Before I know it, I am crying as I drive down the interstate. A deep longing has surfaced. I imagine singing it to my own daughter one day and pray, *Dear God, give me a little girl to sing this to someday.*

Dream a dream of you and me
And dream how happy we can be
Dream a dream of something new
He can make your dream come true

Cause when God thought of you and me
A long, long time ago
We were only make-believe
Until He made us so...

Go on and dream a dream
Make your plans, but
Put them in much bigger hands
Every dream will not come true
But I know the best ones do

Cause when I thought of you and me
A long, long time ago
You were only make-believe
Until He made you so...
Go on and Dream a Dream

"Dream a Dream" © 1998 Skin Horse, Inc. (ASCAP) by Billy Sprague.
Used by permission.

Nineteen springs later, Emmaline Willow Grace is born—the right audience and answer to my prayer.

FEBRUARY 1980...About 2:00 A.M. I wake up with a tickle deep in the back of my throat. Instantly I know it's that cough coming back, the same cough I have had on and off every winter since I caught severe bronchitis in Iceland in 1975. It always starts this way. The tickle. Then the catch when I take a deep breath, followed by congestion which turns into a full-blown, sleep-depriving hack that lasts for weeks. This time I have had it. I am angry. Sitting up in bed in the dark I ask God in irritated tones to PLEASE heal this cough. *I know You can. You can do anything. So will You PLEASE? In Jesus' name.* I go back to sleep.

The next afternoon I realize the tickle is not there. It will be back that night I figure. But the next day, there is no tickle. It takes me three days to consider myself healed. Even longer to believe it. The tickle is not there. And the chronic "walking bronchitis," as one doctor called it, never returns. Answered prayer? Or a virus unable to thrive in an angry host?

THE NEXT YEAR... I fall in love with a young woman I want—more than anything—to spend my life with. She falls in love with me. And out of love. And back in love with her last boyfriend. I pray every night and day for a year that her heart will turn again to me. It doesn't. They marry the next year.

Request denied.

FALL 1983... I am sitting in church for a Wednesday evening service. The pastor invites anyone with a need for physical healing to the front. A three-year-old-shoulder pain is plaguing me again. I have self-diagnosed it as a pinched nerve or muscle damage, originally injured hanging Sheetrock overhead in the spring of 1980. Any fatigue or overuse of that muscle between my right shoulder and neck makes it burn and seize up. I walk to the front, and somebody I don't know lays a hand on my shoulder and prays. I thank them and return to my seat.

This time it takes me several months to realize the problem is gone. To this day it has never hurt me again.

SPRING 1987... My dear friend Anita comes down with cancer. Breast cancer. I pray. Hundreds pray. *Dear God, heal her. Give her strength to endure till healing comes. Give the doctors wisdom. Thy will be done. In Jesus' name.* The more we pray the worse the prognosis. Mastectomy. Chemotherapy. Anita loses her hair.

Anita survived that terrible year. After the thunder of that storm, there's still a light in her eyes. And she shines it on everyone, especially her grandchildren.

APRIL 12, 1988...Climbing the stairs at my home, I collapse in tears. I am terribly lonely. For someone to share my life with. I have so many friends. But no "someone." I scribble down a prayer.

how many nights
must I climb the stairs alone—
dragging my heart up
like a stone—
spilling tears
into my hands—
begging the same
old line again?

how many pieces
must be chipped away—
until there is nothing
left to break—
but only an open
wound that bleeds—
making me free
at last to need?

where is the touch
that will ransom the years—
strip my soul
of its thin veneer—
expose my naked
cringing mind—
and embrace my body
like a clinging vine?

please
how many
please
how many more?
please

tell me
please...please...please
"Please" by Billy Sprague. © 1988 Skin Horse, Inc. Used by permission.

Anne Frank said it well: "A person can be lonely even if he is loved by many people, because he is still not the 'One and Only' to anyone." (Monday, December 27, 1943). My One and Only is still some years down the road. And she is not who I think.

SATURDAY, NOVEMBER 18, 1989...In one week the woman I intend to marry and I will make our engagement official at her home. We will be married next spring. Today she stands beside her car about to drive several hours to surprise me. An older woman standing with her says a quick prayer for "traveling mercies." Nine miles down the road RosaLynn is killed in a head-on collision. I am marooned. Again. This time on an island of grief.

For the next year my main prayers are, *Dear God, keep me going* and *protect me from evil.* By which I mean extreme, unhealthy behavior—in the short term—sleepless exhaustion, drinking, even suicide. And in the long term—bitterness, cynicism, unbelief. I survive. With a little help from my friends. With a lot of help from my friends. And no doubt, their prayers. I survive that year, but do not thrive. For nine months I take up smoking, initially to keep me awake on long drives. I see too many sunrises, flicking cigarette butts into the backyard wondering if thriving is possible.

JULY 1992, BARCELONA, SPAIN...I am a guest artist at an outreach during the Olympics. One of the speakers delivers a talk asking the question: What do we do with our personal pain, which we all have, in regard to our mission in life? Do we get well and then get on with our calling? Or do we respond to our calling and get well along the way? His counsel is the latter—get well along the way. We are all wounded. If we wait until we are well to be fit for our mission, life will be over. He concludes by asking us to turn to two others near us and ask for prayer for a very specific pain in our life. I turn to my Dutch friend Tjiebbo who knows me from two previous trips together in Sweden. I tell him I am coming back to life, functional and even thriving, able to enjoy so much and be useful and productive. But I still carry a fisted knot in my soul about RosaLynn's death. No doubt it is part anger, bitterness, confusion, and a sense of betrayal or unrightness about it. And I don't know how to untie it. He prays two sentences. *"Dear Lord, don't let Billy's memories remain anchors that he has to drag along. Turn them to treasures he can carry with him."* I begin to feel the warm tears gather in my eyes and then drip onto my folded hands. I weep gently. No tumult. No great upheaval.

That's all Tjiebbo prays. We sit in silence for a minute or so. He then counsels me to recheck and let go of any unspoken "vows" I may have made like "remaining single" or "finding a manageable level of melancholy" instead of coming fully back to the land of the living. (Thoreau called it "quiet desperation.")

In less than fifteen minutes I am different. Lighter. The knot in my soul is gone. I take a deeper breath than I have taken in over two years.

The most surprising thing of all is what replaced the knot. Gratitude. I was actually grateful. For RosaLynn. For knowing her. The time we had. And I am thankful for the tenacious love of so many along the way. And thankful to God, who in those moments answered so many prayers.

SATURDAY OCTOBER 22, 1994...I am standing at the front of a church. Next to me is my One and Only, Kellie. We are dressed in our finest. Most of my "please" prayer of April 12, 1988, is about to be answered. The pastor declares us husband and wife, and then prays to God to bless our marriage and the children we will have.

I don't know how much or which prayers influence or change God's mind. I am aware that the Bible says, "The Lord is near. Do not be anxious about anything, but in everything, by prayer and petition, with thanksgiving, present your requests to God. And the peace of God, which transcends all understanding, will guard your hearts and your minds in Christ Jesus" (Philippians 4:5-7 NIV). Perhaps, as C.S. Lewis maintained, prayer may have more to do with influencing me than God anyway.

I still pray for traveling mercies when a friend leaves on a trip. I pray for troubled marriages to be mended. Some of them are, and some end in divorce. In that event, we pray for their kids or, *Dear God, don't let their wounds be anchors they have to drag along. Turn them to teachers and treasures they can carry with them.*

We pray over meals. At bedtime. *Dear God, watch over our Willow and Wyatt in the night. By Your angels keep them safe 'til morning light and make their spirits soft and bright. In Jesus' name, Amen.* More and more I pray part or all of what Jesus prayed. *Our Father in heaven...*

PRAYER IS STILL A BULLETIN BOARD where I post memos to the Almighty. It is not a chess game where I negotiate to get God to see or do things my way. He knows how it looks through my eyes. He knows how to manage a universe. Prayer isn't a way to see things like He does. It's a refuge. An oasis of spiritual life. When I don't go there, I dry up. And brown. Like my yard.

I don't go very long without water. Sometimes, though, I neglect or avoid prayer deliberately, like ignoring my wife or a friend because of an issue I don't want to face. But the restless, unnatural isolation of life as a lone ranger draws me back like a thirst. Thirst for intimacy, I suppose. For nearness, acceptance, consolation. And sometimes in prayer, the lightness and calm euphoria return.

The longer I live the shorter my prayers become. At least the spoken part. Sometimes it's just stargazing and saying, "Thanks for the evening, it was heavenly." Prayer becomes more listening than petitioning. It's like sitting by a stream. Watching the movement. Unable to read the hieroglyphic of light on the surface but consoled by it nonetheless. "I pour my heart out like water," the prophet Jeremiah said. Sometimes in tears. Sometimes in anger or confusion. Often in gratitude. Often in silence. Always in longing. I wait. The river bends toward me. Or I am moved toward it—toward the presence of God. Whenever this happens the current carries me. To deep, still water. And I green.

# 11

# Rivers of Pride

*He that is proud eats up himself. Pride is his own glass, his own trumpet, his own chronicle; and whatever praises itself but in the deed, devours the deed in the praise.*

SHAKESPEARE
*Troilus and Cressida*

ONE OF MY FAVORITE HOBBIES IS *judging people. I find I have a real knack, more like a gift really, for seeing what is wrong with other people.*

That's not me talking now. It's Adam Gardener, my alter-ego. Sometimes he speaks without checking with me first. Whenever that happens in front of a group of people I try to cover for him by saying, "I'm sorry, did I say that out loud?"

Most of the time Adam is benign and playfully entertaining. But he's always candid. He likes to dress up his opinion, the "truth," he calls it, in exaggeration and stories and metaphors.

A great admirer of Mark Twain, he encourages me from time to time to purchase an all-white suit. So far, I have resisted.

Sometimes, Adam can be raw and biting. He likes to think that what he lacks in sensitivity, he more than makes up for in honesty. Not surprisingly, he considers me too sensitive to what others think of me, and therefore willing to sacrifice candor for civility. He makes me nervous.

Having said all that, I knew that in the process of writing an entire book it would be impossible to keep Adam entirely muffled, so I have agreed to let him have his say, briefly, for the purposes of this chapter.

*As I was saying, I first discovered this "gift" in third grade. There was this kid named Tommy whose head looked like someone had mashed in both sides so it reminded me of one of those big angel fish, narrow coming straight at you but big and round from the side view. Tommy used to throw rocks at me at recess. Even then I knew he was mean because he was insecure about being so different. Now I wonder if he wasn't also envious of my nice big round head.*

*Over the years I have honed my gift to a razor edge. One of the great evidences of this is the virtually limitless resource of labels I have been able to create for categorizing all manner of, shall we say, sinners, to use an archaic but judgment-drenched word. Time does not allow me to trot out the entire list but suffice it to say from "atheist" to "zealot," "fundamentalist" to "liberal," "dweeb" to "fancy pants," I can in an instant discern the deficit and spray on the appropriate label like graffiti in the air. I find it an especially fine tool for clarifying between "us" and "them."*

*I am particularly insightful when it comes to morality, especially the morality of others. With the sword of the Good Book in hand I became equipped and qualified to slice and dice those who miss the mark by miles or millimeters, while at the same time leaving myself enough room to appear holy and yet satisfy any appetite that might otherwise go unfed under my more stringent application of the moral code to everyone else. Not that I ever pick up and throw actual stones like Tommy did. That would be, for lack of a modern word, wrong. Or, to use a modern term, intolerant, for lack of a decisive word. No, I find attitudes and words a sufficient arsenal. Let me give you an example.*

*It has been said—or if it hasn't then I'll say it now—that Pride is the mother's milk of the arrogant. Now you take most high-dollar entrepreneurs, and all politicians and Hollywood purveyors of smut, who fatten themselves daily at the bosom of Pride. The hypnotic mantra of "The American Way" has rendered them immune to the clarity provided by truth and justice, decency and compassion. Their common diet is Pride, the great justifier and qualifier.*

*For instance, in matters of Truth they contend, "You shall know the selective truth and the selective truth will set you free, a) free to select certain parts of it to which you will adhere, and b) free to select those who do not measure up to the selected truths applied to them." In other words, their truth is relative. Their justice is for sale. They regard decency as a squeaky shackle forged by phobia-riddled Puritans. And their idea of compassion is a red ribbon worn at awards ceremonies; all the while, in the name of their gods—art, power and pleasure—they portray and/or live as sexually irresponsible, i.e., "liberated" characters. Only the ravages of disease, bankruptcy, and death itself will ever humble them. And then again, it may not. It may only silence them like Citizen Kane.*

*Did any of that make you angry? Then the arrow of truth may have found a bull's-eye. Did any of it feel righteous and good going down? If so, then you may have the gift, too.*

Thank you, Adam.

My point here, and Adam's too, I think, is this: One of the great proofs that we are more than the sum of our biological parts is pride. No other species suffers from this. We call a family of lions a "pride" but that is only a projection of our own nobility blended with a voracious inclination to savagery. Lions have no pride, as such. They are driven by instinct. They do not look at their own reflection in the waterhole in the morning to see what kind of mane day they are having.

WE ARE THE ONLY SPECIES DRIVEN by rivers of pride. Its headwaters are in Eden and its current moves through every gene pool on the planet. It courses through us like blood, but cannot be isolated like platelets.

Pride roars and struts like a lion, but draw close enough to feel its breath and you will see it is only the airbrushed face of fear that cringes in the recesses of us all. It is the wizard's screen and fireworks display, a diversion meant to hide our (my) fear of exposure (see, I even try to hide in parentheses), weakness, failure, duplicity, inadequacy, and ultimately, our mortality.

FOR THE MAJORITY OF US, LIFE IS an exercise in humility. God knew we would have pride issues. (Again, if you are an atheist or Darwinian evolutionist, please forgive what must by now be an irritating presumption of a deity or, in your view, my insufficiently corroborated theist mythology). As I was saying, God knew we would have pride issues. So He provided certain curatives along the way like helplessness at birth, pimples at puberty, marriage for the long haul, aging in general, incontinence in particular, vomiting, diarrhea, death, and (in my case) golf. We, on the other hand resist the therapy with all manner of hypocrisy, blind spots, denial, rationalization, reinterpretation (commonly known as "spin"), bigotry, materialism, nationalism, ethnocentrism, racism (in fact most isms), and cosmetic surgery, just to name a prominent handful.

ONE OF THE LESS INVASIVE REMEDIES for pride is the rosy-cheeked cousin of humiliation, embarrassment. There is nothing like humiliation to shrink certain malignancies of pride, such as stealing, lying, gossip, and the more venial sins, but a little embarrassment helps the medicine go down. I can illustrate this with two episodes.

GROWING UP IN THE GREAT STATE of Texas, where there is no shortage of pride, a friend and I once became partners in a scheme to make extra spending money. On our way home from school, we noticed (I think Glen noticed it first...yes, I'm sure it was him) that a lot of garage doors were left open. In many of those garages stood cases of empty pop bottles. We decided (it was Glen's idea) to liberate those bottles, a case at a time, and redeem them for hard currency, which we did. After a couple of weeks, we amassed literally more than a dozen dollars, each. Nothing emboldens like success, so we became brazen, daylight bandits. I continued to spread denial, hypocrisy, and rationalization liberally over my conscience (enough to steal Coke bottles, but not tools or lawn mowers). However, my cure was soon to come.

One afternoon, I walked confidently into an open garage, directly over to a stack of Coke cases, bent down and picked the top one up. At that moment the door to the house opened. I stood up, still holding the bottles, and locked eyes with the lady of the house. I turned momentarily to stone. Her expression of surprise and confusion is still etched in my brain. She glanced down at the bottles, then gave me the look a lioness gives a jackal. In an instant I was transported thousands of years back in time to a treeless savanna on the western plains running for my life from a saber-toothed tiger and dressed only in my shame.

After that day, my spending money came from my paper route and working at the golf course. I was cured. Temporarily. I have learned that pride is the most clever virus, able to reconstitute itself from a mere scrap of opportunity.

Many years later in a land called…The South…a combination of humiliation and embarrassment applied its healing properties to me again.

The license plate on my truck had been expired for over two months. The reason? An extensive out-of-town touring schedule. That and sheer procrastination. I called the renewal office and told them my road story. I was advised that if I drove down to the main office, I could pay for nine months instead of a full twelve and save some money, about 14 dollars as I recall. Excellent, I thought.

So, off I went. Stood in line. Relayed my story again to an attractive, animated, red-headed, gum-chewing woman behind the counter who slid the proper forms in my direction. One short form said something quite legal sounding like: "Upon penalty of perjury I swear that I have not driven said vehicle between such and such date and today." I did a quick mental stutter step and asked the lady the purpose for this document. She explained that it was a legal declaration to the state that the vehicle had been completely out of use. I instantly thought to myself—*I have been in and out of town and, of course, driven it some, but very little.* Something in me did a quick assessment of the situation and flashed an answer to the question in my brain, "Yes, it is a falsehood to sign this." But only a technical, trivial falsehood of invisible consequence, I rationalized. And I signed my name in the space provided. The boisterous lady completed the transaction, and I left with a renewed license in hand at a savings of more than a dozen dollars.

Driving home the inner dialogue began. *I just signed my name to a lie. Sure, I've lied before. But I never signed my name to one. Don't be paranoid, it's just a license plate. No one's ever gonna know. No one will ever pull that paper out of the state files and bring it to anyone's attention. Better pull into that auto parts store. I need a few things. Quart of oil. Car wax. Grease and guilt remover.* The voice returned. *Don't be ridiculous. You are not going back down there. Let it go. What are you gonna*

*say? I lied? No, I'll just say there's been a mistake on my renewal
and I need to redo it.*

I left the auto parts store and drove back to the license
office. I was relieved to catch them in a lull. No lines. So, step-
ping up to the counter in front of the same lady, I began to
explain. Yes, I was in a little earlier. There's a mistake on my
renewal. Could I redo it for an entire year, etc. She looked
confused. Eyed me. Scanned the papers, all the while giving
her gum a severe workout. Her jaw paused, and a knowing
look came across her face like a lioness stumbling across a help-
less newborn gazelle. She turned to the room full of ladies
manning the computers at a dozen desks and announced in
her finest sarcasm, "Hey girls, (smack, smack) we got an
honest man here. He lied about not driving his truck and now
his conscience is bothering him." The laughter reverberated
around the drab marble and plaster office (a drabness that only
government can design at great cost). I was suddenly transported to a treeless savanna somewhere in the steamy subcon-
tinent where I was encircled by hyenas and wearing only my
honesty.

The leader of the pack enjoyed her moment. I was easy
prey. Ultimately, though, I had the more savory experience.

I squirmed under the good-natured taunts of her and her
pack, expecting an animated Disney musical moment to break
out until, at one point during the transaction, she slid the
signed legal declaration back across the counter and allowed
me to tear it up. The relief I felt supplied the armor to survive
the embarrassment and proved to be the payoff. We completed
our business, and I quickly exited, feeling lighter and ener-
gized, like Opie Taylor when his pa, Andy Griffith, was proud
of him for doing the right thing.

I took two life lessons from this episode: one, if possible,
conduct all government business on time by mail; and two,
everyone has his price. That day for a brief, regrettable
moment, the sale price of my integrity was about 14 dollars.

Even now, pride may be driving me (as in chauffeuring, but at least back-seat driving). Relaying only these two stories of my lesser demons or minor flaws is motivated (on some level) by a desire to portray myself as a man of hyper-sensitive conscience and unswerving will, and is perhaps an effort to paint a picture of impeccable moral character (a reality more remote than Mona Lisa laughing). I am none of these things. That day in the license office, was I more concerned with being honest or appearing honest, by making sure no signed evidence existed to prove otherwise? Even if my motivations in that instance were pure, to describe it now creates an opportunity for pride to feed even on humility. Such is its ravenous nature. Pride has no shame.

But there is beauty in its role in the drama of our lives. Pride always knows its cue. It enters before a fall. And falling makes us look up. It adjusts our lens and perspective, to see things as they really are. To see ourselves as we really are. Fragile spirits in temporary housing. Treasures in jars of clay. Solomon said pride goes before destruction (Proverbs 16:18 NASB), but it can also go before an awakening.

WHICH BRINGS ME BACK TO ADAM Gardener, For a long time now, I have wanted to cast him in a one-man play called, "The Rise and Fall of Adam Gardener," in which he would play the role of spokesman for our entire species. Who better suited? He would have all the lines, no one would interrupt or edit him, and he loves the spotlight. An actor of the caliber of Dustin Hoffman or the late George C. Scott would portray him.

The first half of the play, I imagine Adam retelling his life story from its humble beginnings as an orphan abandoned in a beautiful garden to his current position of worldwide power and influence. How he endured persecution, famine, war, a long season of darkness and superstition, ultimately finding, mostly by sheer force of will, enlightenment and prosperity.

His oratory would be passionate, witty, and wry as he weaves his tale, resplendent in a snow-white suit à la Mark Twain, complete with lighted cigar. After intermission he would retake the stage dressed in an equally splendid jet-black suit, light a pipe, and crack-up the already spellbound audience with the opening line,

"One of my favorite hobbies is judging people. I find I have a real knack, more like a gift really, for seeing what is wrong with other people." Then he would hold forth much as he has just now. For his finale I picture him holding a large, blood-red apple in his raised hand and saying:

"I have tasted paradise. I know the bitterness of the knowledge of good and evil. I have harvested a bounty from the desert of rejection. My seed have become fathers of nations. I have eaten from the fruit of my own accomplishments and savored life. I have peered into the vast unknown and stood before it unafraid."

At this point, Adam takes a large bite from the apple with a loud crunch and begins to choke on it. He tries to dislodge it but cannot. Attempting to remain calm, he takes a sip from a glass of wine poured earlier during a segment on his extraordinary vision for sowing and reaping. He fumbles the glass, drops, and break its. Pointing to his throat, he waves off any help from off stage, giving them an OK sign. He pounds his chest with both fists. The audience is frozen, uncertain if this is part of the script or a real crisis. No one moves to help. Frantic, Mr. Gardener stumbles toward the audience, his face purple from the strain. With both hands at his throat his eyelids flicker and then, for just a moment, he stands motionless in the spotlight, a puzzled look of fear and sadness on his face. Like a giant tree he tips forward, falls on the stage, and lies motionless. Several people from backstage rush to him. The curtain closes. Behind it are the sounds of commotion and running feet. The audience members hang in a suspended disbelief. Surely not, they think.

After a tense two minutes, relief arrives when the curtain rises to reveal a very much alive Adam Gardener. He appears disheveled yet poised. At the end of thunderous applause, the actor invites everyone to retire to the lobby for a cup of apple cider, compliments of the house. More applause. And all the sons and daughters of Adam exit back to the drama of their own lives, divided over whether the ending was part of the play or part of life.

RELAX, ADAM, IT'S JUST MY WAY of putting words in *your* mouth for a change. (I love to play with his mind sometimes.)

# 12

# And Justice for All

*If the universe is not governed by an absolute goodness, then all our efforts are in the long run hopeless. But if it is, then we are making ourselves enemies to that goodness every day.*

C.S. LEWIS
*Mere Christianity*

WHEN I WAS IN THE FOURTH OR FIFTH grade, my friend Ken and I took an afternoon job delivering a sales advertisement for Big B Discount store. The owner didn't mail them probably for the same reason he was in the discount business. It was cheaper to hire two kids to go door to door than pay the post office two cents per flyer. (I think we got fifty cents for every hundred delivered.) If no one was home at a house, we stuck the flyer in the screen door or laid it on the porch. We took opposite sides of the street and raced each other to see how fast we could empty our bags.

From out of nowhere, a police car pulled up, an officer called us both over to the car, and asked what we were doing and who hired us. He must have been a cousin of Deputy Barney Fife, a real by-the-book cop, because the next thing I knew he was saying something about having to take us down to the station because we were breaking some city ordinance about door-to-door solicitation and littering. I was really scared. I had never been in trouble, big or otherwise, or in a police car. I remember thinking, "Can he really do this? Something is not right." But who was I to question his authority? So the deputy put us both in the back seat of his car, hauled us down to the station, and made us sit around sweating what would happen next. After an hour or so, our dads showed up to sort it out and take us home. I still don't know exactly what it was all about. (I'll bet Andy Taylor would have gotten to the bottom of it and discovered that we left a flyer at the home of a merchant who competed with Big B Discount, and he called Deputy Gung-ho at the police station to put a stop to the advertising.)

IN THE SIXTH GRADE, I WAS walking home one day. Just past the corner of a wooden fence on my right, a big guy jumped out, knocked me down, and jumped on me. We rolled around in the dirt, him ending up on top and me trying to dislodge him. I weighed about sixty-five pounds. He weighed well over a hundred. He roughed me up a little and then took off. He didn't hurt me much really. Years later, I heard he became a preacher. Perhaps he had a change of heart. Still, I like to picture him out there wrestling sinners into submission from his bully pulpit. I still don't know why he ambushed me that day.

MY SOPHOMORE YEAR OF HIGH SCHOOL, just after lunch, my friend Glen (my partner in the Coke bottle crime) and I came upstairs out of the cafeteria. The rule was you had to go on outside, weather permitting, and wait for the bell to ring for the next class. At the top of the stairs, we turned right. The principal, "Red" Hooper, was sitting on the left across from the candy machines. He had a stern look on his face to match the marine flat-top on his head. Glen and I stopped at the machines to make a selection. From behind us, Mr. Hooper said, "Sprague, Carter, get your candy and move on outside before I haul you down to the office." He sounded irritated. Maybe it was gruff playfulness and I misread it. But it struck me as such an unreasonable, bullying tone. And I spoke before I could think (a habit a long time in breaking).

"But we're not doing anything, you can't do that," I said. I think I was actually thinking, "Can he do that?" but it didn't come out like that.

I honestly did not intend to sound impertinent, and perhaps Mr. Hooper misread *my* tone. But the next thing I knew he had me by the back of the neck escorting me down the long and not-winding linoleum hallway to his office. I weighed a hundred pounds. He weighed nearly twice that. He sat me in a hard chair in his office, looked at a couple of memos, and gave a secretary some instructions about something, while letting me sweat out what might come next. Finally, he made some small talk about what kind of school year I was having, but the sentence that still sticks in my head is this: He looked me in the eye and said, "I can do anything I want to around here, is that clear?"

"Yes, sir."

"Now get outa here."

I did.

I DON'T REALLY BELIEVE MR. HOOPER meant "anything" to mean torture or murder. It was just his way of making sure I knew where my freedom ended and his authority began. Maybe his sensitive trigger that day came from an altercation with his wife that morning, and my perceived insolence pushed him over the edge into re-exerting his power base, at least in his work environment. Any number of things could have been going on.

But I still wish, in all three of those circumstances, that some Andy Griffith—or better yet, John Wayne—would have shown up on the scene and given me what every human in our species cries out for. One of those "things you just know." Justice.

I like to picture John Wayne walking in to Mr. Hooper's office and saying, "Well, 'scuse me, Red. You're out of line here. I'll be takin' the boy with me now. You got a problem with that?"

"N-n-no, Mr. Wayne," the suddenly contrite Mr. Hooper would say.

"C'mon, son. Le'me buy you a Butterfinger." And as we exit together, me and John, I mean, Mr. Wayne, he turns back to the principal and says, "Well I sure hope this clears things up and I don't hear about a backlash or any more trouble from this. I wouldn't like that at all, pilgrim. Understood?"

"Perfectly, Mr. Wayne. Nice to meet you. I loved you in *Red River.* Have a nice day, Billy."

But no one showed up. And each of these incidents left indelible red flags in my psyche about this world and the reality of injustice.

Granted, these were minor abrasions. I personally have suffered very little injustice compared to so many. I grew up with a fair-minded father and a loving mother. I was white (still am), fairly bright, and innocuously low profile, or at least I thought so until my senior year (weighing in at 123 pounds), when I was nominated (but not elected) in the Best Personality category.

I have very little idea what it feels like to grow up in America as a target of injustice, especially as most minorities experience it. An African-American friend of mine has tried to explain to me how overt and subtle the injustices of racism can be. I can see it. I watched it boil over in the '60s, but I have not lived my life as the target of it. No matter what we said back then in the pledge of allegiance every morning, this was not yet a land of "liberty and justice for all." It's still not. Neither is the world at large.

The only time I actually became the focus of true, overt, personal persecution, discrimination, and injustice, based on who I am or what I believe, was on my first trip to Amsterdam in July of 1986. (Certainly, on most talk shows in the last 25 years I have felt "lumped in" with Christians in general as small-minded, intolerant, anti-everything, regressive, judgmental, religious bigots. But that kind of cultural, first-amendment-guaranteed bashing remains remote and can be tuned out with the red button on the remote control.)

I was standing in front of the Queen's palace, just a few blocks from Anne Frank's hiding place. A group of missionaries had just performed a wordless play set to music depicting the state of the world, human nature, and Christ's sacrifice. I was with the group but not in the drama. After it concluded, my part was to hand out a small piece of paper announcing a concert that night at which I was to be a performer. The play ended, and I began to pass out the flyer. (I must've blocked out the trouble I had as a kid handing out flyers.)

A few feet from me, a man began to shout in German or Dutch. The only part I understood was the anger and the English obscenities. Before I knew it, he had chosen me as the main target of his rant against Christianity, Christians, and Americans. It turned out he not only cursed skillfully in English, he also spoke it fluently. He positioned himself well within my comfort zone and began to hurl language in my face that seemed like the artillery barrage that precedes an actual attack. Any second, I knew he was going to deck me. I weighed about 170 pounds. He was wiry, about 150 to 160 pounds. For the first time in my life I actually outweighed an oppressor. But he was obviously a lot more committed to violence than I was. (Where is John Wayne when you need him?)

He continued to unleash a torrent of venomous fury and didn't give me a chance to say a word or try out my nearly award-winning personality on him. I can joke about it now but I was truly afraid for my safety. By God's grace or the sheer number of people at my side, he didn't hit me. His tirade went on between five and ten minutes (a month in dog years) and then he stormed off through the crowd stopping every few yards (metres in European) to scowl and hurl verbal javelins in our direction.

Later, as I reflected on my trip, which included my first visit to Anne Frank's hiding place, and my first reading of her diary, the incident in Damm Square struck me with greater force. The face full of fury that had launched such an attack on me was the same face that came through the door and dragged away Anne and her family and friends and millions of Jews, non-conforming Christians, and other "undesirables" to the death camps. It was the same fury that slaughtered and burned Native Africans in South Africa and African-Americans in the South where I live. More recently, it was the same face that shot an entire family of nine Moslems in Kosovo, including a two-year-old boy, and threw them all down a well. It is the same blind rage that burns in hate sites on the Internet and incites teenagers to slaughter God-believing fellow students and then think, like Hitler and some of his dark henchmen, that they can escape justice in the safety of death. And it is the same fear and hate-contorted face that crucified Christ.

On this planet, we share an awareness of injustice because we have a deep, foundational sense that there ought to be justice. There is a standard that defines right and wrong, good and evil. We may differ on where that line is but we do not differ that there is a line.

It's hard to tell just when the night becomes the day
The golden moment when the darkness rolls away
But there is a moment none the less
And in the region of the heart there is a place
A golden charter that should not be erased
It is the marrow, the moral core
That I cannot ignore

Within the scheme of things
Well, I know where I stand
My convictions they define who I am
Some move the boundaries at any cost but
There is a line I will not cross
No riding on the fence, no alibis
No building on the sands of compromise
I won't be borrowed and I can't be bought
There is a line, I will not cross

Ask the ocean where the water meets the land
And he will tell you it depends on where you stand
You're neither right or wrong
But in the fathoms of the soul that won't ring true
Cause truth is more than an imposing point of view
It rises above the changing tide
Sure as the morning sky

"There is a Line" © 1993 Careers-BMG Music Publishing, Inc. (BMI)
Beucap (ASCAP) All rights on behalf of Magic Beans Music admin. by Careers-BMG
Magic Beans, BMI/Skin Horse, Inc. (ASCAP) Kirkpatrick/Sprague.
Used by permission. Recorded by Susan Ashton on *Susan Ashton* for Sparrow Records.

THERE IS A LINE, A STANDARD. And we all want a representative of that standard. John Wayne or Andy Griffith. The U.S. Supreme Court or the World Court, it doesn't matter. But where did they get their sense of justice and right to enforce it? The prophet Isaiah seems pretty sure about it. "I [the LORD] will make justice the measuring line" (Isaiah 28:17 NASB).

Fyodor Dostoyevsky, C.S. Lewis, Solomon, and others do a much better job of describing what I am getting at—that the sense of justice and injustice in us all is evidence of an objective standard and a Creator of that standard. So I will recommend them to you and be brief.

Every time I see actual film footage of World War II or a documentary about Hitler and the great atrocities he and others engineered in such an evil, organized way that, with venom aforethought, targeted Anne Frank and millions of others for annihilation, I think, and usually say out loud to my television, "There's got to be a hell." I know that sounds politically incorrect in the extreme, and not "nice" in keeping with the current fashion of tolerance, but this is not a completely nice world. David agonized about this in Psalm 73. Speaking of the not nice, he said:

> Pride is their necklace;
> they clothe themselves with violence.
> From their callous hearts comes iniquity;
> the evil conceits of their minds know no limits.
> They scoff, and speak with malice;
> in their arrogance they threaten oppression.
> Their mouths lay claim to heaven,
> and their tongues take possession of the earth.
>
> When I tried to understand all this,
> it was oppressive to me,
> till I entered the sanctuary of God;
> then I understood their final destiny.
>
> Surely you place them on slippery ground;
> you cast them down to ruin.
> How suddenly they are destroyed,
> completely swept away by terrors!
> As a dream when one awakes,
> so, when you arise, O Lord,
> you will despise them as fantasies.

Psalm 73: 6-9, 16-20 NIV

The violent, chaotic dream I had as a kid pointed to the reality of evil. Even though the soft glow from Mayberry and other early TV shows tried to paint a world without dark, black evil, the air-raid drills in elementary school were a real-world alarm announcing the opposite—that hate, and injustice, brutality, and destruction are also bound up in being human.

No one has yet isolated the gene or developed a drug, like the "soma" everyone was required to take in *Brave New World*, to cure us or keep the dark side in us at bay. Karl Marx, and others, would do away with religion, the "opiate of the masses" as he saw it, that "drugged" society into passivity and regression. And replace it with what? Constitutions and pledges of allegiance to them? I don't see evil receding much because of the enlightened, even brilliant documents written by men of the highest character and intent. That only seems an attempt to shift the base of authority and trust from a higher source to the minds of men. For this world, that may be effective to the degree that men can agree. (Astounding and troubling as it may be, there are those who still herald Hitler as a hero and adopt the same brutal measuring stick as the Third Reich.) But in the next realm, if there is a next, the measuring line will not be in human hands. "God himself is judge" (Psalm 50:6 NIV).

IF WE ARE ETERNAL BEINGS AND there is a heaven, and so much argues for it, then, in order for mercy and grace to exist, it seems there must be a hell. (Huxley suggested that this planet might be hell for another world. But I don't think so. For at least two reasons—ice cream and sex. Ain't no hell got either one.) Among whatever agonies hell holds—perpetual hunger, thirst, and pain, or unrelenting shame and sorrow— the greatest must be this—exclusion from heaven.

> With you *[God]* the wicked cannot dwell.
> The arrogant cannot stand in your presence;

you hate all who do wrong.
You destroy those who tell lies;
  bloodthirsty and deceitful men the LORD abhors.

Psalm 5:4-6 NIV

That's more than a little troubling, because I have been wicked, arrogant, and done wrong. I have told lies. Perhaps even been bloodthirsty. And certainly deceitful. I'm glad the Psalmist didn't stop there. He went on to name the other measuring stick God uses. "But I, by your great *mercy*, will come into your house" (Psalm 5:7 NIV). That's a murderer and adulterer talking. Apparently mercy will be shown to the undeserving. I want in on that.

IN THIS WORLD, EVERYONE DOES NOT get justice or mercy. But everyone wants it. Justice for others. Mercy for ourselves. There are strong indicators in this world that, in the next one, the Maker of the standard will apply it to the living and the dead. And both justice and mercy will be perfectly applied to every soul by the One who is perfect in both.

# 13

# Harvesting a
# Vacant Lot

*I reason, Earth is short—*
*And Anguish—absolute—*
*And many hurt,*
*But, what of that?*

*I reason, we could die—*
*The best Vitality*
*Cannot excel Decay,*
*But what of that?*

*I reason, that in Heaven—*
*Somehow, it will be even—*
*Some new Equation, given—*
*But, what of that?*

EMILY DICKINSON

*I'll tell you "what of that," Emily. It hurts. That's what. Life hurts.*
And I think that's exactly what my favorite American poet
was getting at. In the face of suffering—logic, reality, even the
promises of Heaven can all turn into Job's ineffectual friends,
especially when doled out by well-meaning, quick-fix, Alice in
Wonderland, evangelical platitudinites. The numbing cocoon

of loss or pain cannot be brushed aside by glib references to Romans 8:28—"All things work together for good..." (NASB) or "This too shall pass," or the sardonic homespun quip, "Oh, well, in a hundred years we'll all be dead anyway."

True as those are, when pain prowls inside you like a panther, the shortest verse in the New Testament becomes the mightiest. "Jesus wept." He knew life was brief. He knew anguish and death and loss were inescapable realities in this world. He knew He Himself would "excel decay," beat death, and thereby bring a "new Equation" into the cosmos by factoring in resurrection and eternal life for all who would believe. He knew all this. And yet Jesus stood at the graveside of His dear friend Lazarus, knowing He would raise him from the grave in ten minutes, and wept. He wept bitterly. It hurt.

IN NOVEMBER OF 1989, I STOOD by the graveside of RosaLynn. We would have been married the next spring. But in a split second, in the time it takes to peek around a van to see if the road is clear to pass, she was gone. Divine ricochet? Guardian angel on a smoke break?

I know life is short. I know death comes to us all. I carry the unshakable belief and hope that in heaven "it will all be even." But on this side, there is real loss and for so many who must trudge through a winter of loss, not only from death but loss of any kind, there is a cruel, mathematic-like net deficit in the equation of life. "The masses of men lead lives of quiet desperation," Thoreau put it. And to avoid deficit living, he moved off into the woods.

I moved to a vacant lot, at least emotionally. All the dreams and plans and longings were leveled to the horizon and beyond. The season changed to winter inside my heart and refused spring for over two years. Out of the sheer pain and shock, the *whys* and *what ifs*, the sleepless nights, the wrestling match with God, and the test of faith, two questions emerged. The first, simply one of survival: Is there a way through? The second, which came much later: Is there a way back? To life? To feeling? To joy? Or would I become one among the masses, quietly desperate, subtly (or openly) cynical, trudging toward the ultimate and only relief, death and heaven beyond?

IT IS ONLY BY THE GRACE OF GOD and many heavyweight friends that I can now answer yes to both questions. There was no quick fix. There is no short answer. I can only give some glimpses of that long and winding road.

I FOUND MYSELF IN THE SAME wrestling match that C.S. Lewis described in *A Grief Observed*. He wrote, "Not that I am in much danger of ceasing to believe in God. The real danger is of coming to believe such dreadful things about Him.... What reason have we, except our own desperate wishes, to believe that God is, by any standard we can conceive, 'good'?"[1]

Since early 1988, I have been singing a song I wrote called "La Vie" (Life). In it are two lines in French, which I was told the Christians in France use quite often. "La vie est dure, mais Dieu est bon." Life is hard but God is good. Like Lewis I wondered, "Doesn't all the...evidence suggest exactly the opposite?" Doesn't RosaLynn's death and all the net deficit in the hurting world prove a net deficit in the God I had leaned on for so many years?

Looking back, I can see the test of faith more clearly. It was a not-so-simple fill-in-the-blank. Life is hard but God is _____? (I always hated fill-in-the-blank tests, so I'll give you some multiple choices.)

Several weeks after the accident, at Christmas, one of my brothers came to my bedside and said, "Why don't you go do what you want now? You've done it God's way and look what you get." He was angry for me. I lay there lifeless, my head shaven from grief, a truly sad sight. I remember listlessly saying to him, "Where else am I gonna go? Should I sell books in the airports with the Krishnas? I wouldn't look good in saffron sheets." His remark filled in the blank with a logical, cynical answer based on the apparent evidence, and many people conclude just this: Life is hard but God is *unreliable*.

JUST AFTER CHRISTMAS OF THAT YEAR, I was standing by Rose's grave with her father, one of her brothers, and one of her sisters. The winter wind was slicing through us, but we hardly noticed. A car stopped a short way from us, and a man got out. He was over fifty, short, his hair and bushy mustache graying. He looked a little like "old man winter" himself. When he saw who we were, he headed directly for Rose's father, his old brown coat flying open, both arms extended wide, and tears streaming down his face. As he approached, his eyes never left Dr. Olivares. He spoke in anguish raising his voice to carry into the wind, which was loud in the branches above us. And he said this, "I'm so sorry you have to hurt this way." They were the first words that pierced my numb heart and I will never forget them. Only later I found out that the man was also a doctor, a colleague of Rose's father, and had lost his own wife the previous year.

Through all the impenetrable silence from heaven, the hollow days, the listless hours, the deep, unanswered agonies, the "mad midnight moments" as Lewis called them, I carried the image of that man and his words, I suppose because I must know that God, though silent, hurts, too. Jesus wept. That doesn't unravel the why's and what if's but it changes everything. Life is hard but God is *tender-hearted* (or at least not indifferent or unmoved).

IN FEBRUARY OF 1990, I SANG and spoke at my first event since Rose died. A singles' conference—the last place I wanted to be, especially grieving over a dead fiancée. After one of my sessions, a brave and tender soul came up to speak with me. She offered me the first scripture that actually stuck to my soul. It was from Ecclesiastes, not the perkiest book of the

Bible. "It is better to go to a house of mourning than to go to a house of feasting, because that is the end of every man, and the living takes it to heart" (Ecclesiastes 7:2 NASB). She explained that it is not more fun in the house of mourning but it is better because the perspective is as crystal clear as it gets in this world. There is a certain creeping cluelessness about prosperity that deep loss will not allow. She said that my perspective would be keener and more farsighted than it had ever been. If perspective came with such a high price tag, I wasn't sure I wanted it. But she had the credibility of a calm soul, acquainted with suffering, yet not sad. I took in her words like a starving pilgrim. Life is hard but God is *wise*.

LATER THAT SPRING, I REDISCOVERED the poetry of another single-by-circumstance person, Emily Dickinson. I ran into lines like, "There is a pain so utter it swallows substance up" (#599), and "You left me, Sire, two Legacies/A Legacy of Love/...You left me Boundaries of Pain/Capacious as the Sea/ Between Eternity and Time/ Your Consciousness—and Me (#644), and "How happy I was if I could forget/To remember how sad I am" (#898). Here was someone who knew loss. I read her poetry daily and for three weeks dug up worms morning and night for a little robin that had fallen out of a nest into my backyard until, shortly after I released Pocotera (Littlewing), I found this one:

> If I can stop one heart from breaking
> I shall not live in vain
> If I can ease one Life the Aching
> Or cool one Pain
>
> Or help one fainting Robin
> Unto his Nest again
> I shall not live in Vain. (#919)

Just when I was wondering if God had vacated the universe for happier climes. I actually laughed. Real laughter. And cleansing tears.

EMILY SAID MORE: "I shall know why—when Time is over/And I have ceased to wonder why/Christ will explain each separate anguish/ In the fair schoolroom of the sky" (#193), and "This World is not Conclusion/A Species stands beyond/Invisible, as Music/But positive, as Sound..." (#501). But what of that? A little bird? A long dead poet of passion and faith? Evidence? Of what? How would Emily fill in the blank? Life is hard but God is *visible in all circumstances* (#820) or simply "*our Old Neighbor*" (#623).

THAT SUMMER A FRIEND'S grandmother wrote me. During World War II, Marion Brady had faced what so many had. The khaki-colored car pulled up in front of her house. The somber officer came to the door and handed her the dreaded telegram that began, "We regret to inform you..." Her husband was killed at sea. She never remarried, but raised her children and endured. Some of her words to me were these, "The pain will be less on the cutting edge in time. You have been given great gifts by God. You can use them in dedication and devotion to your young lady, and the more you use them, the better you will feel."

I never met Mrs. Brady, though we spoke on the telephone and wrote a couple of times. She had a delightful, even outrageous, sense of humor. She helped show me there was a way through. The more I sang and wrote and wrestled, the better I felt. Mrs. Brady died and joined Mr. Brady in December of 1993. She filled in the blank something like this: Life is hard but God is *faithful and practical.*

DOZENS OF SMALL INCIDENTS, flashes of understanding, ("twigs of evidence" as Emily called them) occurred along the way. Like a song by Chris Rea called "Tell Me There's a Heaven" in which a little girl sees a lot of battered and dying people on TV and asks her daddy:

> Tell me there's a heaven
> Tell me that it's true
> Tell me there's a reason
> Why I'm seeing what I do
> Tell me there's a heaven
> Where all those people go
> Tell me they're all happy now
> Papa, tell me that it's so.
> <small>"Tell Me There's a Heaven" © 1989 Warren/Chappell Music (ASCAP) by Chris Rea. Used by permission.</small>

The song seems to say: Life is hard and God is *not forthcoming*.

Later, one Sunday afternoon on a rebroadcast of a William F. Buckley interview with Malcolm Muggeridge, the topic was faith. Mr. Muggeridge quoted King Lear as one of the most concise definitions of faith he had ever heard. In the final act when Lear's daughter Cordelia is wondering why all the suffering was inflicted on her father, the blinded King tells her we must "take upon ourselves the mystery of things" (V. iii.16). Life is hard but God is *deliberately unhelpful for His own inscrutable reasons.*

About the same time, something I had read many times struck me with greater force than ever—Paul's letter to the Thessalonians. "We do not want you to be ignorant about those who fall asleep, or to grieve like the rest of men, who have no hope..." etc. (1 Thessalonians 4:13-18 NIV). Life is hard but God is *sovereign (not nervous, has a specific, long-range plan that is not irreparably derailed by the exit, untimely or otherwise, of any one person from the planet).*

I began to find twigs of evidence in such unexpected places. While reading the letters of Vincent Van Gogh, I found this statement of faith: "Sometimes the pilot of a ship can use a storm to make headway, instead of being wrecked by it." And I painted it in large gold letters on my bedroom wall so I could read it every morning. Life is hard but God is *able and resourceful.*

ABOUT A YEAR AND A HALF had passed when, after a concert in Florida, I met a woman who came to hear my music because she had heard my story. She was curious to know how I was making it. Her fiancé had died of a heart attack 15 years earlier. She had found a way through, but not a way back. We talked for several hours. In college she had studied philosophy and decided existentialism was the bravest system of thought and belief with which to face reality—the "what you see is all you get" approach. We compared notes on the landscape of our tragedies. After 15 years, she was still hard as nails and mad at the cosmos. So, I asked her, "How is that philosophy working for you?"

She said something I will never forget: "I have found that applying philosophy to the reality of death is like swallowing an elephant. It just won't go down." She had spent 15 long, painful years in self-protection and wounded isolation. She had not loved again nor married. She had filled in the blank—Life is hard but God is *absent.*

AS TIME TRUDGED ON, I DISCOVERED there really was a way through. I wrote songs, traveled, made homemade ice cream, took missions trips, scuba dived, grew tomatoes, and recorded an album, *Torn Between Two Worlds.* The question remained: Is there a way back? My friends were still wondering. And so was I. Was it possible for all the "twigs of evidence" scattered along the way to take root, sprout, and blossom again in such a vacant lot? Life is hard but is God *that good a gardener?*

IN AMSTERDAM ON THE WAY home from a missions trip to Sweden, one evening I talked with a young woman, Yvette, whom I met in July of 1986 and hadn't seen in nearly six years. Her zeal for God and characteristic Dutch frankness helped me turn a silent corner, though she probably doesn't know it. During our conversation she looked up at me from the floor where she sat and blurted out, "So, Billy, will you ever marry?" I squirmed a bit and dodged the question, saying basically—I don't know and my heart is not at that place yet and I don't know the future. Then with great tenderness, she looked up at me and said, "Well, Billy, I know at least one person in heaven who wants you to be very happy." I couldn't fight that kind of eternal perspective. I knew immediately Yvette was right. And the undodgeable reality of that worked on my stiff heart like strong hands. The blood flowed into abandoned places inside me like rain on dry ground. Life is hard but *God, and the citizens of heaven, are for us.*

I HAVE ALREADY DESCRIBED HOW, later that year, in July, I went to Barcelona for a missions trip, and another conversation relandscaped my insides in a major way. I am still so grateful to my Dutch friend, Tjiebbo, (who is as discerning as and more frank than Yvette). I described to him the twisted knot inside me about Rose's abrupt, and what I sometimes called rude, departure from the planet. It was a hard-to-reach mess of tangled long-term sorrow and disappointment with life and the way God runs, or allows, the universe to run. After his short prayer asking God to turn my memories into treasures, not anchors, and the deep comfort and release I experienced, how could I resign myself to deficit living? I still remember taking in a breath of life all the way down to my toenails. And, as I already described, the knot was gone. Life is hard but God is *redeeming (and He knows tangled knots better than all the Boy Scouts and sailors in the world).*

SINCE THEN, I HAVE WRITTEN hundreds of songs, traveled, made homemade ice cream, taken missions trips, scuba dived, grown tomatoes, completed another album, *The Wind & the Wave,* started oil painting, and fallen in love with and married a precious, life-savoring woman named Kellie, surely one of the bravest people on the planet. At this writing, we have two twigs of merciful evidence of heaven's influence and reality, Willow and Wyatt.

GOD DID WHAT I THOUGHT BEYOND the reaches of even His death-defying power. He harvested my vacant lot. In the test of faith, He filled in the blank with His own goodness. And I am convinced that the way we fill in that blank, "Life is hard but God is ____," largely determines the quality of our lives, the peace of our minds, the health of our hearts, the calm of our souls, and the pace of our steps.

Emily was right. Earth is short. Anguish is absolute. Vincent was right. A good ship's pilot can use a storm to make headway. Paul was right, too. We grieve over real loss with real tears, but with real hope. And Marion was right. And so were Yvette and Tjiebbo and Shakespeare. And my favorite Hebrew poet said it better than I ever could:

> [God] reached down from on high and took hold of me;
>     he drew me out of deep waters.
>
> He rescued me from my powerful enemy,
>     from my foes, who were too strong for me.
>
> They confronted me in the day of my disaster,
>     but the LORD was my support.
>
> He brought me out into a spacious place;
>     he rescued me because he delighted in me.
>                               Psalm 18:16-19 NIV

King David would agree with the French believer: Life is hard but God is *bon, si bon (good, very good).*

# 14

# Seeing Is Deceiving

*I tot a taw a putty tat.*

<small>TWEETY BIRD</small>

THE LITTLE ROBIN I MENTIONED earlier was the first of a small flock of homeless fledglings that fell into my backyard. Every May, for five years in a row, beginning with Littlewing, I rescued young birds, mostly robins, that dropped out of the trees. I don't know if they were victims of sibling rivalry, clumsy, or simply overeager to test their wings, but there they were, grounded, unairworthy, and easy prey for my cat and four or five others that patrolled the neighborhood. In fact, their snarls of competition over a downed bird more than once alerted me to the situation.

I always felt like the hero rushing in (if not from Mount Olympus, then at least from my perch at the top of the food chain), rescuing the frightened baby bird, while the evil cats sulked and cried foul.

Sometimes the damage was already done. The bright red blood on the soft breast feathers, or the limp, broken wing told me this little one would not survive to fly. The sinking feeling always vied with acceptance. Having dove hunted a few times in high school, I knew how to end the agony of the doomed ones in a moment.

Still, the bravado of their protests, even at my rescuer hands, and the futile struggle against my grasp reminded me of my own time in the grip of grief not long past. And the throbbing pulse of their fear always struck me. If I waited, some grew quiet and still and looked uncomprehendingly up at me. Most kicked and screamed, "No! No!" or "Why? Why?" or whatever baby birds cry.

"Some things happen you can't help," my Grandma Myrtle used to say. This was one of those things.

After I ended a bird's misery, the cats never seemed as interested in a lifeless lump of feathers. I suppose their hunter instinct got shortcircuited by, what must have seemed to them, my unnatural intervention. Their sullen faces always seemed to say, "Humans, they just don't understand." And they are right. (Cats are never wrong. And they need never apologize. No wonder they sleep so well.)

Sometimes in May, though, I found one or several of the little feathered groundlings unharmed, hungry, and typically ungrateful for my assistance. Occasionally a bird's parents, especially robins and bluejays, would squawk and hover around and threaten to call in the Feathered Bureau of Investigation.

The first few years, I attempted to nurture the baby birds in a box on the back porch. Digging up worms was time consuming, so I called a wild animal rescue line to get some advice on care and feeding. They suggested I put them back in a nest if at all possible and let nature take its course. I did, and that worked a few times. But that wasn't always possible, so I became an occasional Florence Nightingale to the orphan bird population. Sparrows, robins, bluejays, starlings, grackles—I took them all in. I tried not to be preferential to the cuter ones, but it's a fact: starling and grackle baby birds are just plain ugly. But I didn't leave them for the cats' amusement. If I couldn't locate a likely nest, they all received the same care.

More often than not, they didn't make it. In the morning I would open the box. And find them. It was always so disappointing. It clashed with the outcome I wanted. It collided with Emily's lines, "'Hope' is the thing with feathers/That perches in the soul/And sings the tune without the words/And never stops—at all"(# 254).

MY SUCCESS WITH THE FIRST robin, Littlewing, had spoiled me. He thrived so well. When I tried to release him from the back deck, he made a short circle and landed on my shoulder. He did this repeatedly. I finally had to drive him to Radnor Lake, a park here in Nashville. Even there, he hopped down a trail for half an hour and would not fly away. Finally, I set him on a lower branch of a small dogwood tree. He looked around, and then, as if a light came on, he leaned forward into the air, made a graceful upward sweep, landed confidently on the shoulder of an old tree, and stood surveying the possibilities of his new world. The last time I saw him he was profiled against the blue sky like a noble symbol of hope on some royal family crest.

IN THE THIRD SPRING, I FOUND a retired man who took in baby birds. So I drove them out to his house. On one trip, a young robin in the box on the seat beside me fully extended its wings, threw its head back, beak wide open in a silent scream and convulsed. Its wings made short, rapid scraping noises on the cardboard as it vibrated. I knew it had eaten nothing in the last two days. I drove faster. The bird was in its death throes. It collapsed and then repeated the contortions and shuddering. It was a tortuous dying swan song. Without the song. It was the most silent agony I have ever seen. When the wave of pain passed, the little robin went limp and waited for the next one. I drove faster and prayed out loud. I hurried to the man's door, and he said what I already knew. It was too late. But he took him in. I drove home.

Some things happen you can't help. A lot of things. Accidents. Calamities. Disasters. Diseases. Death. Sunrise. Sunset.

Sometimes it feels like the whole universe should be cordoned off by yellow crime tape. In one sense, it's nothing less than wholesale slaughter to inflict such agony on creatures unable to opt out of the game. I'm very surprised no one has charged God with creation neglect or even child abuse. What parent, seeing a child in harm's way, would not intervene, especially one with unlimited power to do so? Now that I am a parent, I would do anything to keep my children from harm. But I won't be able to. And whether I like it or understand it or not (and I don't), agony, decay, tragedy, and death are dark strands woven into the fabric of the physical universe. To some degree, this is by God's design, if the words of Jeremiah the prophet are reliable: "Is it not from the mouth of the Most High that both calamities and good things come?" (Lamentations 3:38 NIV). Is the world a cruel Divine terrarium? A tragedy of inexcusable proportions? Where's the sense and the hope in it? What do I tell Willow Grace and Wyatt?

I IMAGINE THE DAY WILL COME when one of my children finds a little bird and wants to rescue it. We will try. And the bird will live or die. And I will say to them, "Some things happen you can't help." And they will begin to learn the hard lesson of dark and light.

How will I explain to them that things are not always what they seem? That there is more going on than meets the eye? How will I let them know that a bird is a flesh-and-blood-and-feather parable, a visible picture of an invisible but nagging and eternal reality?

It's a hard lesson. Real birds fall out of nests and get tormented and killed by real cats. Real birds die. All living things die. But if the spirit exists, hope goes on, singing "the tune without the words—and never stops—at all."

Will they get it? Or will it hit them somewhere down the line someday, perhaps standing in front of Rembrant's painting, *The Return of the Prodigal Son*? Will they see the looming darkness that dominates the canvas but realize it is the light that draws them? That "The light shines in the darkness, but the darkness has not understood it"? (John 1:5 NIV).

The lesson of light and dark hit me again on a hot, sunny day in June of 1999. My studio office is in the backyard. Through the window I saw a dark spot in the grass. At a glance I detected some movement. June was late for a fallen fledging. Most of the baby birds of April and May had grown up and flown away. We had acquired a golden retriever that kept all but our own cat away, but the bird wouldn't last long if Caleb came along.

It looked to be a dark, fairly mature grackle fledgling. I could see it opening and closing its beak in the hot sun, typical of birds trying to vent themselves. It wouldn't last long in the heat. All this went through my mind in a couple of seconds. I hurried outside to the rescue, excited to be of service again.

What I discovered was not a bird (though it rhymes with bird). It was a pile of dog poop. Perched atop it was a medium-sized, intricately ochre-painted butterfly. Its wings moved rhythmically open and closed. I had mistaken it for the beak of the "bird." I burst out laughing. I laughed till I cried. I could not stop laughing. I sat down in the grass and watched the butterfly. With its feet planted firmly in Caleb's ample, daily offering, it sunned itself like a rich tourist on a black volcanic, Hawaiian beach. I laughed some more and said, out loud, to God, or perhaps the angel in charge of butterfly memos that day, "Thanks, I really needed that."

I WILL TRY TO TEACH MY CHILDREN that light is also woven into the fabric of life. And that things are not always what they appear to be. That some things happen you can't help. Some of them are very good. And some of them are hysterical.

# 15

# Let It Be Said

*Live like you'll die tomorrow*
*Die knowing you'll live forever*

RICH MULLINS

MY SONGWRITER FRIEND RICH MULLINS was killed in a car wreck on a Friday night in September of 1997. Eight or nine months later, I had a dream about him.

In the dream, Rich, my wife, Kellie, another friend of mine and Rich's, Don Donahue, troubled actor, Robert Downey, Jr. (go figure), and I were all sitting around a kitchen table, one of those chrome and vinyl diner-types. Rich looked like I rarely saw him. Rested. He radiated health. His dark eyes shone with the boyish glint that always vied with the dark, manic sage that also lived within him and drove him to mine musical nuggets of glory from the daily stream of living. I asked him about some melody line in one of his songs. Rich just started laughing. My real-life awareness of his death intruded, and I said to him, "Are you here?" meaning, "Are you really here?"

He only laughed more. He had a great laugh. It was so good to hear it again. I was suddenly compelled to hug him. So, I did...and kept hugging him while he laughed. He never said a word. Kellie and Don wondered what was up until Robert Downey, Jr. said, "I guess sometimes you miss someone ahead of time."

I still don't know exactly what that means (like some lines in Rich's songs). I woke up wanting to re-enter that dream to hear Rich laugh some more, but I was already back in the stream of living and couldn't reverse the current.

IN SO MANY WAYS, RICH LIVED out of sync. His inner clock was not set to Greenwich mean time. Sometimes his ways looked like procrastination, selfishness, dreaminess, or distraction, and, no doubt, some of this was the case. But there was another factor. Rich lived ahead of time. In fact, he wrote some songs looking back from beyond death, with titles like "The World As Best As I Remember It" and lines like "When I look back on the stars/it'll be like a candlelight in Central Park/And it won't break my heart to say goodbye" (from the song "Elijah" on his self-titled recording, *Rich Mullins* Reunion Records, 1987).

I've never met anyone like him, with such a heightened daily awareness of the brevity of life and the passion to use the time you have to be involved in things that matter.

Most would write off Rich's lifestyle as peculiar to an "artistic" temperament. But he didn't live for the art he created. It was just something in him that had to get out. And the influence that heaven had on him didn't make him of no earthly use, either. In fact, instead of pursuing the level of notoriety and financial rewards that his music created for him, he aimed his life away from those, preferring instead to give his energies and gifts to mission work and teaching kids. He lived on far less than he made. When he died, he was teaching and living on a Native American reservation in Arizona. He never married. He owned very little.

To my thinking, Rich didn't stay here long enough. But he sure burned bright while he was here.

Pain and joy lived side by side in Rich, if not comfortably, then compatibly. It was no surprise to him that at any moment joy could give way to deep sorrow or suffering, and vice versa. That made him seem very old in one sense—weathered and resolute. But in a flash he would crack a joke and laugh or ask, "Do you want to hear a new song?" Then, after playing some amazing, powerful piece, he would look at you like a six-year-old and ask, "Do you like it? You really like it?" I always did.

HE AND I USED TO HAVE A RUNNING argument about Solomon. Rich would side with Solomon and doggedly maintain that everything is meaningless. I, being more foolish, would argue against Solomon, supposedly the wisest person who ever lived, that he became a depressed old man who had too many women and lost sight of the whole picture.

Rich would say, "Maybe he was depressed because he did see the whole picture," and then laugh. Our debate, as best as I can remember it, would go something like this.

"How can everything be meaningless if, like Genesis says, God created the world and said it was good?" A good point, I thought.

Rich would maintain his stance, focus it away from "creation" to the view that everything we *do* is in vain.

"Then why do you do anything?" I would counter.

"Because God expects me to, out of love for Him," Rich once said. "And out of love for Him, I want to."

"Then, that gives it meaning," I said, in a checkmate move, or so I thought.

"No, that only shows that for that moment my heart is in the right place, but everything I do is still of no value. It's only the love that matters."

Usually he wasn't trying to be semantically slippery. Although, most of the time he was not content to allow anyone to have very much completely figured out and pinned down. For Rich, the uncertainty of life was a fertile place for faith to grow. Keeping off-balance was a means of not settling in on a planet he was only visiting.

I thought I had him when I said, "If everything is in vain or meaningless, then how are you able to laugh and enjoy life so much?"

"Because Solomon said if you're unlucky enough to be born into this world of suffering, about the best you can do is enjoy your work, enjoy what you eat and drink, and keep God's commandments."

To which I said sarcastically, "Now there's a religion to attract the masses already leading lives of quiet desperation."

"I'll drink to that," he came back with a chuckle. "Anyone hungry?" And we would move the discussion to a nearby restaurant.

The only consensus we ever arrived at is a point that Rich made. If Solomon were the wisest man who ever lived, maybe he was playing devil's or skeptic's advocate for anyone who believes that this life "under the sun" is all there is. From a point of view without an eternal connection, the meaning drains out of everything. And Solomon was hammering the point home by taking that side of the argument. I could raise a glass to that as well.

When the time came to leave, many times Rich's parting words were the same, a paraphrase of Solomon, "Be good, but not too good. Why ruin yourself?" (Ecclesiastes 7:16). It sounded like he was giving me, and himself, permission to be mischievous. It may have been his wry way of having the last word.

*Hey, Rich, is it meaningless that I miss you? What's the matter? No comeback for that?* Guess I finally have the last word on something. That's meaningless consolation.

Whether he was at any given moment whimsical or sardonic, the sheer force of who Rich was always made me more alive. I always felt challenged and awakened, and drawn closer to the pulse of life after a little time spent with him. His music still has that effect on me. It probably boils down to the passion created from him living what he believed. And he lived like he might die the next day, so he chose to be involved in things that really matter. The kids on the reservation must really miss him.

LIKE RICH MULLINS, THE PEOPLE I know personally or only watch from a distance who receive the highest admiration of their peers, some of them the applause of the whole world, are those who, on a very day-to-day level, live what they believe—not perfectly, but persistently. And the common thread is this: They turned away from living just for themselves. At some point they turned to something bigger than themselves. And longer than their own lives.

Like Virginia Saucier, my Sunday school teacher in high school, who radiated joy and faith. Ron Lowe, my youth director during that same period, who fed me on a steady diet of affirmation. Ed Cartwright, an elder at our church. I worked in his dry cleaning business one summer. He was the kindest, do-for-others person, even if they were covered in the stains of irritability and bad manners. He almost always had a glint of playfulness in his eyes and told me many times, "You've got it. You're a natural." Mother Teresa, the saint of Calcutta, who viewed and treated the invisible of the world with dignity and mercy. My own mother, the saint of my childhood, who gave her days to raising five children. My own wife, who trades so much of herself for our two little ones. Princess Di, who walked into and out of a fairy-tale life and whose sudden death reminded so many of things that really matter. The nurses and doctors in pediatric ICU where our son, Wyatt, spent his first two weeks on the planet, who give such tender care to all babies of all blood types and races, in all conditions.

THIS IS A VERY SHORT LIST OF PEOPLE who believe we are
more than the sum of our parts. At some point, they chose to
lean the weight of their existence on that belief, and it shaped
the course and character of their lives. And they make us all
more alive. To what really matters.

They all have something in common. They discovered one
of the great ironies of living inside an organism where self-
preservation is a central motivator. They learned the secret so
eclipsed by a culture whose primary engine is self-interest.
They learned somewhere (probably from someone who was
already living the secret) that the key to life is giving it away.
In the face of so many unknowns, they at least know why they
are here.

*Hey, Rich. Want to hear a new song?*

> Living in a world of joy and agony
> Can leave you staring at the moon
>     At night and asking why
> Are we briefly here to simply
> Chase whatever fills our empty souls
> Until the candle of our time goes out
>     Or is the answer hidden
>     In the hand that's always giving...without a doubt
>
> Oh, to be here living every minute
> To see the glory in it and to face
> The world awakened and discover
> The key to life is giving it away
> To be is to be here for each other
>
> The saddest part of loving is to watch someone
> Losing their way somewhere
>     Between to be or not to be
> In a world of hearts in tatters
> Fragile souls forget what matters most
> And turn away pretending not to see

But you showed us that every breath
Of life we breathe is sacred...and meant to be

You took the art of living to extreme
And showed the world what loving means
And it's so beautiful to be...living for each other

Oh, to be here living every minute
To see the glory in it and to face
The world awakened and discover
The key to life is giving it away
To be is to be here for each other

"To Be Here" © 1999 Acuff-Rose BMI / Skin Horse, Inc.
(ASCAP) Joe Beck / Billy Sprague. Used by permission.

If Rich were still here, I know my next question in our discussion would be: "If it's only the love that matters then, the things we do out of love are not meaningless or in vain, right?"

THE REAL-LIFE OLIVER WENDELL HOLMES said, "Most people die with the music still inside of them." I'm sure Rich had more songs inside, but he got a whole lot of music out of him before he left. He played his part. So did Mother Teresa. And Ed Cartwright. And the beat goes on.

*Hey, Rich. Want to hear another song? I always sing it with you in mind. (OK, with Mother Teresa, and Ed Cartwright, and a few others in mind, too.) Hope you like it.*

Who will remember you were here?
And hold your memory dear?
I will—through all the years
One day in Glory's hallowed halls
The heavenly applause
Will roll—for you because

You fed the lake of love
You filled the cup of peace
And gladly poured your heart out for

One aching soul to ease
You raised a glass of laughter at
The wonder of it all
And learned to rain forgiveness
By standing in the waterfall
You carried help from heaven's well
To cool one fevered brow
And emptied your life in the river that runs
And returns to the heart of God
Where you are sailing now

Will told us all the world's a stage
We've all a part to play
So speak—your lines with grace
Though all the world is not impressed
The ones who know you best
Will stand—and—let it be said

"Let It Be Said" © 1998 Skin Horse, Inc.
(ASCAP) Billy Sprague. Used by permission.

It seems only fitting and fair to let Rich have the last word.

And now the storm is fading
And the night is through
And everything you sent to shake me
From my dreams they come to wake me
In the love I find in you
And now the morning comes

And I can see the things that really matter
Are the wings you send to gather me
To my home
To my home
I'm going home

"Home" © 1996 BMG Songs, Inc. (ASCAP) Rich Mullins.
From the recording *winds of heaven, stuff of earth*
Reunion Records 1988. Used by permission.

# 16

# Life Is a
# Long Goodbye

*Farewell, Adios*
*And all the goodbye words*
*That hurt us the most*
*They will be obsolete*
*No more bon voyage, no arrivederci*
*There's no need for auf Wiedersehen*
*When there's nowhere to go*
*To get back from again*
*And I'll look at you for an eon or two*
*Or three or four or more, and say*
*Hello, Hello*
*How I missed you so*
*And then we'll know forever*
*And have ourselves a long hello*

from "Heaven Is a Long Hello" © 1991 Skin Horse, Inc.
Bencap Music (ASCAP) Billy Sprague. Used by permission.

MYRTLE PAYNE WAS BORN July 31, 1895, as Myrtle Lee
Hefley. She was the youngest of nine children. The "runt of
the litter" she called herself. She outlived them all. By decades.
But not because she wanted to.

My grandmother met her true love, Will Sprague, skating on Big Pond in northwest Arkansas. He was fifteen. She was two years younger. They were too poor to buy skates so they just slid around on their shoes. Will held her hand on the ice that day. "And that was it," she told me. He was the one. Seven years later, in 1916, they were married.

Life was hard. They were Oklahoma farmers, inseparable co-workers keeping a place running. "He couldn't drive a nail less I held it for him," Myrtle would "complain." That was her style, scrappy and playfully put out with everyone. It was a likable mask for the huge sorrows in her life, protecting her private pain while allowing her natural wit and buoyancy to come through muted and endearing.

Will liked to do more than just work. He played the fiddle. In fact, one time he made his monthly trip into town for various supplies with twenty dollars, a lot of money in those days, and was supposed to buy flour, sugar, and other staples. Instead, he ran into a man selling a fiddle, spent the whole twenty on it, and borrowed five dollars from Myrtle's sister, Bonnie, so he wouldn't show up back home with no provisions at all. Myrtle was not pleased. My dad still has the fiddle. It was made in Cremona, Italy, in 1733 by a student of Stradavarius—at least that's what the handwritten label inside says, and probably what the fiddle seller showed Will.

To hear Myrtle tell it, life consisted mainly of work. "Had chores to do from sunup to sundown. That's just how it was," she said. But they faced it together.

They had a sweet arrangement about who got up first and lit the fire in the stove. Will took the winter shift. Myrtle managed the warmer months. The duty changed hands like this. In autumn when Myrtle woke up and saw frost on the window, she rolled over, poked Will in the ribs, and said, "First frost, Will. Your turn." Then, in the spring, the morning would come when Will would roll over, pat her on the backside, and say, "First whippoorwill, Myrtle. Your turn." Her shift was longer. But his was colder. Seven decades later, in 1994, I borrowed this bit of personal history for part of a wedding song to my own bride, Kellie.

> The yellow sun climbs
> Into the blue, blue sky
> The silver moon looks on in gratitude
> Stronger than darkness
> Sure as the morning light
> Will be my love for you
>
> Through all the days of
> Blossoms and whippoorwills
> This love will bloom and grow
> So deep and true
> And when the frost lies
> Upon the windowsill
> This flame will burn for you
>
> You bring the flowers
> I'll light the fire
> And as the journey goes
> Heavenly Father
> You hold us close
> For we know it's all for You
>
> When life is over
> And I must fly away
> If it's allowed I'll come
> To help you through
> And keep the promise
> I make to you today
> I will be there for you

"For You" © 1994 Skin Horse, Inc. (ASCAP) Billy Sprague. Used by permission.

Two years into their marriage, on March 20, 1918, their little girl, Mary Violet, was born. Three and a half years later, she died. At home, where most dying happened back then. On the evening of the night she succumbed to the strangling cough and fever of diphtheria, Will went out to the general store to get a few things. From her bed, Violet called out to him in a weak voice, "Daddy, get me some gum. Get me some gum?" Will said all right but came home without it. He forgot. Violet was disappointed but listless from the fever. She died sometime in the night, September 26, 1921. Myrtle told me that for years, every time they got near the subject, Will went quiet and said the same thing, "I can't believe I forgot Violet's gum."

I could never really imagine Myrtle's pain until our Willow Grace was born. At seventeen months old, she came down with the croup the day Kellie went into the hospital to deliver Wyatt. To hear her labored breathing over the monitor was agonizing. One night, between bouts of coughing, she called out repeatedly, in her little sleepy, ragged voice, "Daddee, Daddee, Daddee." I hurried to her room, scooped her up, and held her. Standing in the darkness with my sick little girl in my arms a vision of my grandfather Will doing the same thing seventy-eight years earlier came into focus. I broke. It was only a fraction of the pain Will and Myrtle carried for the rest of their lives—she for seventy-six more years. He bore it not nearly as long.

Six years later, in their tenth year of marriage, Will died in Myrtle's arms. A few weeks earlier, he had done what she had begged him not to—gone down the road to visit a little boy who had typhus. The boy was burning up from the fever. His room was on the sunny side of the house, so Will built an awning above the window to shade his room. Myrtle never understood that typhus is not usually transmitted by human contact. Will probably caught it drinking from a stream

or pond while hunting. She always believed the act of kindness
cost Will his life. And her happiness.

When the fever put him in bed, his brothers, five of them,
came around and stayed around eating and drinking and
playing cards with him. "They wore Will out," she said, "He
couldn't rest." She never forgave them.

At four o'clock on the afternoon of October 13, 1926, Will
couldn't get his breath. He tried to say something to Myrtle,
couldn't, turned his face away in frustration, and died. She was
six months pregnant with my father. All of her life she wondered what he wanted to say. Every time she told that story,
she said, "My life ended that day." But she didn't die.

SIXTY-THREE YEARS LATER, I PLAYED guitar with four of
my Grandpa Will's five brothers in a dirt floor garage in Col-
gate, Oklahoma. Mac, the oldest, and only non-player and
non-drinker, lived the longest, dying at age one-hundred-one
and a half. Sanford and Corbett strummed along while Ted,
the youngest brother, sawed on a fiddle. He reminded me of
Picasso's painting *The Old Guitarist*. He drooped in a losing
battle with gravity, his skin hanging on his bones like an old
suit. Ted was blinded in the South Pacific in World War II
from drinking "torpedo juice," methyl alcohol. He seemed a
little under the influence that day. Fact is, a couple of them had
been moonshiners early in the century. They told me Will was
the best musician among them.

"Will could burn up a fiddle," Mac told me. Even when
they were still boys, Will used to wake the family up some
mornings with a lively rendition of one of his two favorites,
"Sailor's Hornpipe" or "Turkey in the Straw" (which Will
always insisted was called "Natchez Under the Levee").

My dad and I went over to Mac's afterward to look at
family pictures. He was the self-appointed historian of the
family. I remember one wide panoramic photo, black-and-
white of course, of a baptism on the banks of a river. The

women all wore long white dresses, the men dark suits or over-alls. A preacher stood in the water with the next or most recent convert. It was taken very early in the 1900s. The preacher was my great grandfather, Will's dad.

Myrtle once mentioned her own baptism to me. It seems about six weeks before Will died, they went to a preachin' and were baptized in a pond in eastern Oklahoma. That was in August of 1926. She was four months pregnant. I was curious to know what made her decide to get "dunked" that day. What I really wanted to know was what in particular the preacher said to make her do it. Grandma responded in her frank, concise way with what she thought should be obvious to anyone, "Didn't want to go to hell, a course." We both laughed.

"I guess that's good a reason as any," I said.

I ASKED GRANDMA ONCE, after my fiancée died in a car wreck, how she made it through Will's death. "I prayed every night the sun wouldn't come up. But it did. You keep on going. You have to. You got no choice."

She kept going. In 1931, she married Alfred Raspberry Payne. They called him A.R. for obvious reasons. She asked him to marry her. The Depression was making a hard life even harder. "I needed a home and father for Bill (my dad). And Alfred wanted a family," she told me.

Alfred was fourteen years older than Myrtle. A churchgoing man. I don't remember him ever saying a word to me. I suppose he did, but I don't remember it. He drank his coffee from a saucer and sat in his rocker. If five grandchildren running around his little place ever irritated him he didn't show it.

A.R was not a musician. In fact, according to Grandma, he wouldn't allow music in the house. Early on, Myrtle had a radio that she bought with part of the thousand dollars from Will's insurance money. One day Alfred took it out in the yard and smashed it. He was a member of a denomination that disallowed instruments on the grounds that they might get you in trouble with God because they weren't specifically mentioned in the Bible, at least not in the New Testament. I'm glad he didn't apply that same caution to cars, because after he died on his birthday in 1964 of a heart attack, my dad drove A.R.'s '55 Chevy back to our house in Texas, and my brother Barry and I shared it during high school. I did my share of "parking," as we used to call it, in that car—with the radio tuned to KOMA out of Oklahoma City. A.R. would not have approved.

I wrote some of Grandma's life into the "Life is hard but God is good" song I mentioned earlier called "La Vie."

My grandmother Myrtle has outlasted two husbands
All of her sisters, brothers, and cousins
And wonders why she's still alive
But she smiles and will tell you
That trouble won't kill you
Cause if it did she would have died

O, La Vie est dure, that much is sure
Mais Dieu est bon, si bon
Through the fire and the rain
I call Him by name
And when the night is long
I remember mais Dieu est bon

"La Vie" © 1996 BMG Songs, Inc. (ASCAP)/Skin Horse, Inc. (ASCAP)
All rights on behalf of Skin Horse, Inc. admin. by BMG Songs
Billy Sprague. Used by permission.

Despite her protests, I'm pretty sure Grandma liked it. She prominently displayed the beautiful calligraphy of the lyric a friend of mine made for her. And after that, whenever she told me a story from her life, she chided me in a snarling smile that made her words mean exactly the opposite by saying, "Now, don't you put that in a song, honey boy." (Sometimes she called me "Honey Boy." I really miss that.)

THE TIMES GRANDMA SPOKE OF Alfred she would say, "I kept my vow. I respected Alfred. But I loved Will." And whenever she spoke of seeing them in heaven, Grandma chuckled but made it very clear that she hoped Alfred understood but she wanted to see Will first.

In Alfred's defense, my dad says he was a good father to him, the only father he ever knew. And I wonder if maybe it was not the music that made A.R. break the radio that day. Maybe it was a link Myrtle still had to Will. Maybe Alfred knew he didn't occupy as dear a place in her heart. Maybe in a moment of anger, Myrtle reminded him of that, or just telegraphed it in subtle, or not so subtle, ways. Subtle was not generally her style.

All this came back like an echo in my own life. When I was pursuing my wife, she was determined not to end up in a strangely parallel scenario. Like Alfred, I am 15 years older than her. Like Will, I am a musical man who, like Myrtle, buried someone I loved and had planned to spend my life with. Kellie was not about to walk in Alfred's steps, respected but not loved. She wanted both. And to her credit, subtle is not her style either. She wanted a man with a whole heart, fully alive in this world and not secretly waiting for the afterlife to be reunited with a former love. Her Myrtle-like tenacity helped love me back to life again.

IN REGARD TO "TILL DEATH do you part," Myrtle really did take the longer shift. She outlived Will by seventy years, five months, and four days. But she never fully came alive after he and Violet left. She sent a big part of her heart on ahead. The rest of her stayed here. For my part, I'm glad she did. And I told her, "Grandma, I think you're still here for me. I needed you."

She taught me many things. Directly and indirectly. When we spoke on the phone or in person at her little house, Alfred's house, she always had a practical proverb of some kind, like "Some things happen you can't help," or "Trouble comes to everyone, best be happy while you can." (If Solomon had been born in Oklahoma, he would have put it that way instead of, "When times are good, be happy; but when times are bad, consider: God has made the one as well as the other" Ecclesiastes 7:14 NIV).

Like most of us, Grandma didn't take her own advice. Most of her adult life she worried for a living. "Are you makin' it alright in that music business? Now tell me the truth. You know I'd give any of you kids my last penny. Do you have to travel so much? Those airplanes worry me to death. How is everybody? Now tell me the truth. They won't tell me a thing." And so it went.

For her one hundredth birthday in 1995, I took some of the phrases she used a lot and wrote her a song. The things she taught me directly form the verses. The chorus she taught me, without knowing it, from her life.

> Best be happy while you can
> Grandma said it so off-hand
> The wisdom of a hundred-winter dance
> Best be happy while you can
>
> Some things happen you can't help
> Time and trouble taught her well
> Cry—but let it go—why hurt yourself
> Some things happen you can't help
>
> Lean upon the love of God
> And friends who will be true
> Learn how to fill your heart
> In the solitude
> All the worry in the world
> Cannot a minute buy
> And love will not survive
> Inside a fisted hand
> Best be happy while you can

Trouble comes to everyone
When it does you must go on
Some nights you pray to God hold back the dawn
Trouble comes to everyone

Chorus

After Grandma died I wrote one more verse:

She used to call me "honey boy"
Her style was pleasantly annoyed
One half sorrow—one half wounded joy
She used to call me "honey boy"

Myrtle's long goodbye is over. She has nothing to worry about now. On March 31, 1997, she died peacefully, which had always been her prayer and mine for her. "Some morning I just don't want to wake up."

She and Will and Violet are together. And Alfred, too. And I bet they all understand. And there's plenty of love to go around. If there's a heaven. If not, if this life "under the sun" is all there is, then a kindness of the grave will be forgetting. Forgetting Myrtle, Will, and even my own wife and children. But for now, I remember.

# 17

# Remembering Forever

*Over and over, like a tune—*
*The Recollection plays—*

EMILY DICKINSON

WE, THE LIVING, REMEMBER.

And we can conceive and feel eternity. Does thinking it and feeling it make it so? No. But everyone on the planet shares such a similar longing. The Tihua people of Borneo dig up the bones of their parents and children every year and wash them so their souls may enter the afterlife they call "the prosperous village." And the current generation is relying on those following behind them to do the same to insure their own entrance into paradise. Would Dylan Thomas wash his own father's bones if it enabled a reunion with him in an afterlife? I suspect so. And I suspect even the skeptic, cynic, agnostic, and devout existential atheist carry a kernel of intellectually well-guarded hope that eternity and paradise just might be so. (In her *An Introduction to Jung's Psychology*, Frieda Fordham contends that there are dreams that "can demonstrate—if he will but take notice—to a confirmed agnostic that he is really a believer at heart or lead a renegade back to the faith he has forsaken.")[1]

We, the multitudes, remember.

But is there truth in numbers? The revered psychologist Carl Jung thought so. His concept of a "collective unconscious" has generally unqualified acceptance among modern, educated men. Besides his fascination with dreams (Jung believed that all his dreams were sent by God), he's the fellow who developed the therapeutic device of free association. You say a word, and I say the first thing that comes into my head. "Meat?—Potato." "Mayonnaise?—Mustard." "Life?—Death." "Dough?—Knob." (Obviously an example from the Deep South.)

Jung said there is a realm of psyche that belongs to all mankind, acts and mental patterns shared universally by our species. These occur as archetype images, patterns, and symbols that are often seen in dreams or fantasies and appear as themes in myths, religion, and fairy tales. It's a collective memory bank, a pantry in the psyche stocked with things like wheels, circles, jewels, birds, eggs, a chalice, a divine or magical child, lion kings, Camelot, and heroes and such. (I guess ice cream doesn't qualify as an archetype.)

Jung deduced the existence of a collective unconscious "in part from observations of instinctive behavior"[2] and inferred it "from the obvious traces of mythological images"[3] in our dreams. Isn't his theory an argument for an unseen reality based on a preponderance of psychological data? Or is it merely a high-flying euphemism to set us above and apart from all other merely instinct-driven species? (There's that pride thing again, so easily spotted in others.) Is it only a self-ennobling net of words woven to throw meaning around our finite existence? Is heaven merely a Jungian archetype?

To be fair, and I don't pretend to be an expert on him, Dr. Jung did not denigrate religion. In fact, he pointed to what he called the "religious function" inside us as the best means of pursuing the most significant task any person can achieve, namely, harmony between the conscious and unconscious. (That sounds an awful lot like the seen and unseen worlds to me. Or a strong parallel. I can't imagine a better harmony between life and death, dark and light, than a real Creator, an actual, not mythological, Savior and an ultimate, not archetypal, heaven.) However, he did think the church majored too much on exteriors of religion instead of the interior work of redeeming and harnessing the "shadow" (his new word for the sinful aspect of human nature) inside us and reconciling us via the light of God within our souls.

It seems fewer and fewer people today, at least in my culture, deduce or infer a Creator behind the creation. No doubt, that's largely because, as Jung pointed out, "Science is the tool of the Western mind...it obscures our insight only when it claims that the understanding it conveys is the only kind there is."[4] I suppose to many people, Jesus, and His birth, identity, death, and resurrection are unacceptable "data" processed through a series of sophisticated arguments (made by data-interpreting pragmatists like *Bloom County*'s Oliver Wendell) and deemed to be inadmissible, much like contested blood evidence in a murder trial. It's just too obvious and conclusive. And possibly tampered with by the early witnesses. Therefore inadmissible. I know the first thing that approach would bring to Myrtle's mind, and lips: "Fiddle-faddle."

Does anyone seriously think scientists will someday isolate the "religious function" gene or the "longing for

heaven" center in the double helix of our DNA and cure us of
it?

Until then, I want to meet my Grandpa Will. And his dad.
And see my Aunt Violet's sweet face. I have never even seen a
picture of her. I want to see Alfred and RosaLynn again in that
place where no one is more loved or less dear than anyone else
because everyone is loved so fully. I want to meet my wife's
Grandma Ruth and see my songwriter friend, Rich Mullins,
and have Solomon himself settle that argument once and for
all. And Ed Cartwright. Mother Teresa. Princess Di. Tennessee
Ernie Ford. Frances Bavier and Howard McNair (Aunt Bee
and Floyd, the barber, from *The Andy Griffith Show*). Marion
Brady, whom I only met over the phone. Tom Copeland, my
favorite English professor at Texas Christian University
(TCU). "Satchmo." And Narnia creator, C.S. Lewis. And
maybe chat with him and "Al" Huxley (who both exited the
planet on the same day as JFK, November 22, 1963.). Anne
Frank, and personally thank her for her book. John G. and
Lina Balleu Barnes. Emily Dickinson. Vincent Van Gogh.
Beethoven. Imagine walking up to Mona Lisa and saying,
"Hey, aren't you...?" And she and Nat King Cole laughing
right out loud. And so many others. All laughing right out
loud.

And if, as Emily hoped, "Christ will explain each separate
anguish/In the fair schoolroom of the sky (#193)," I want to
know why Alfred broke the radio. It probably won't even
matter then, but I still would like to know. And I want to
know what Will couldn't say to Myrtle with his last breath.
Was it about forgetting Violet's gum? An apology for buying
the fiddle? Was he frustrated and sad about not being there for
her that winter to get up first and light the fire? Or was he
angry that he would not be here to see his son, my dad, be
born eleven weeks later on January 9, 1927?

I want to spend a long span of eternity saying hello and
remembering the long and winding road together—talking

and remembering it together, maybe over a dish of something cool and divinely rich and creamy, in the sweetness of each other's company and the presence of heaven's Maker. Imagine talking and listening and laughing and singing and seeing how it all fit together in God's grand design, because the Grand Designer will be there. Then again, I wonder if the only memories of this part of the lovely, dangerous road will exclusively be all the things done in love along the way. And the smashed radios and broken hearts won't even come up.

There's only one way I'll ever know these things or see these people—if these words are true, "In my Father's house are many rooms; if it were not so, I would have told you. I am going there to prepare a place for you. And if I go and prepare a place for you, I will come back and take you to be with me" (John 14:2,3 NIV).

I keep going back to that. And to this, too.

> We do not want you to be ignorant about those who fall asleep, or to grieve like the rest of men, who have no hope. We believe [*there's that believing thing again*] that Jesus died and rose again and so we believe that God will bring with Jesus those who have fallen asleep in him. According to the Lord's own word, we tell you that we who are still alive, who are left till the coming of the Lord, will certainly not precede those who have fallen asleep. For the Lord himself will come down from heaven, with a loud command, with the voice of the archangel and with the trumpet call of God, and the dead in Christ will rise first. After that, we who are still alive and left will be caught up together with them in the clouds to meet the Lord in the air. And so we will be with the Lord forever.
>
> (1 Thessalonians 4:13-17 NIV)

I like these words, especially that part about Jesus bringing with Him those who have fallen asleep. That fits with Solomon's words about the spirit returning to God and the body going back to the dust at death (Ecclesiastes 12:7). I like it because it means Myrtle's spirit is with God now. And the wrinkled, age-spotted hands and body she complained about aren't frustrating her anymore. Apparently, her ninety-pound body, sustained so long on a diet of chicken and dumplins, biscuits and gravy, canned peaches, angel food cake, heart medicine, and worry, will be raised (completely overhauled and renewed, "The dead will be raised imperishable, and we will be changed," 1 Corinthians 15:52 NIV) and her spirit rejoined with it to live beyond death.

I love these words. And I wonder if the "voice of the archangel" will sound anything like Nat King Cole. And if the one playing the "trumpet of God" knows any Louis Armstrong tunes. I am drawn to these words because they mean we have not been left behind and forgotten. And they confirm that believing leads to seeing and beholding the intangible.

I HAVE MORE REASON THAN EVER to remain on the planet a while longer. To "drink the days, taste the time," to learn to love well, enjoy my wife, watch my boy and girl grow up, and make memories, music, and ice cream. And to play my part in the scheme of things. Life can be a lovely ride. But I know it can turn on a dime. And probably will. If I can stay as alert and scrappy as Grandma Myrtle, I wouldn't mind staying a whole century like she did, though I know that would include a lot of goodbyes, some longer than others. Odds are, I'm only halfway through this life, but the chorus of "In the Sweet By and By" is already growing sweeter to me. And at every goodbye I will have to return to those words about a place beyond this visible world. And if I should exit before my friends and wife and children (*Please, not after my children—*

there's that prayer thing again), I hope they return to them, too.

For some time now, any number of things can bring those words to mind. A movie. A celebrity death. Certain music. Calamity on the news. A gathering of people who rarely get together. A brilliant sunset. The picture of Grandma in my office. A cemetery. Or especially when I have to pull over and watch a funeral procession pass by, that picture of a great reunion comes to mind. I keep going back to it, like our annual Ceremony of the Golden Scoop, because it tastes good to my soul. And because it bears repeating. Like "Amazing Grace." And a dream in a young boy's head.

# Appendix 1

# Recipe for a Cool Clue to the Meaning of the Universe

*"I like it!"*

WILLOW GRACE'S FIRST SENTENCE
© Sunday January 16, 2000.
Used by permission.

A GREAT SONG IS LIKE GREAT ice cream, but not exactly. Both have universal appeal, but one has high fat content. Both can make your life sweeter and your heart lighter, but one makes the rest of you heavier.

In an effort to enhance the flavor of your own life, I offer my own personal, universally appealing, high-fat rendition.

**Directions**: Blend the sugar, eggs, whipping cream, salt, and vanilla in the big blue bowl. I use a whip. The longer you blend, the fluffier and creamier this gets. I never use an electric blender but experiment to see how blending time affects texture. I myself like the texture to be as dense and deadly as

## Ingredients:

1 cup sugar

4 eggs

½ pint heavy whipping cream

1 pint half-and-half

¼ teaspoon salt

**3 or 4 sloppy tablespoons of Mexican vanilla** (This, above all other ingredients, is the quintessential element in the alchemy of ice cream. Accept no other vanilla. Or forever be tormented by the nagging thought, "I settled for the bronze medal in the ice cream event.")

**2 14-ounce cans of sweetened condensed milk**

½ **gallon whole milk** (skim milk should be considered only by heart patients or heretics)

**1 very big blue bowl** (preferably a crock bowl of considerable age and character, previously owned by at least one grandmother, and purchased by you at a flea market after considerable, congenial haggling over the price)

(Note: this recipe makes five quarts. Adjust the amounts to the capacity of your ice cream maker. Though why anyone would make less than a gallon at a time is beyond me.)

possible. Next add the half-and-half, and sweetened condensed milk (and recycle those cans, please). If the volume of the mixture is too great for the blue bowl, well then, your idea of a big blue bowl and mine are two different things and it's time for another trip to the flea market. In lieu of that, transfer the mixture to the ice cream maker cannister and finish blending.

At this point you have a choice. You may fill the cannister to the guide line (adding whole milk to fill it to about ¾ full) and proceed to create a world-class batch of Mexican Vanilla or follow directions for fruit and flavors (below).

(**Warning**! **Danger!** At this point, Greed and Gluttony will conspire to make you overfill the cannister in an effort to maximize the sheer volume of ice cream. Heed them not. Or the mixture will overexpand, lift the lid and you will deserve the consequence of your avarice—rock salt in your ice cream.)

**Note:** Experiment with these ingredients. For an even richer blend, double or triple the whipping cream and use only half-and-half instead of whole milk to fill the cannister. More milk fat means richer ice cream, smoother texture. Or use only one can of condensed milk and increase the sugar and eggs.

**For fruit flavors**: (Raspberry is my favorite.) Don't add the whole milk yet. Puree at least two cups fresh or frozen raspberries in a blender together with two cups of the Mexican vanilla mixture from the cannister. Blend this potent potion back into the cannister. Now add whole milk (or half and half) up to the guide line. Insert the dasher or paddle. (I actually forgot this important step in my haste one time and an hour and a half later wondered why the ice cream wasn't getting hard. Lesson? In life as it is in making ice cream, you must have your paddle in the water to make progress.) Proceed to freeze the mixture in your ice cream maker. (Your other option is to freeze a batch of basic Mexican vanilla, open the cannister, add the fruit mixture and then let it sit in the freezer two to four hours. This is especially helpful if you enjoy larger chunks of fruit. The larger chunks clog the paddle and prevent the ice cream from freezing in the cannister.)

**For coffee flavors**: Dissolve five or six (or ten, depending on how strong a coffee flavor you prefer) teaspoons of instant coffee into a cup of the Mexican Vanilla mixture from the cannister. Microwave it slightly and stir until fully blended. Add it back to the cannister. You can also use an extremely concentrated cup of expresso, but the more water in the mixture, the less creamy and potentially icy the results will be. (You can counteract this a bit with a little powdered milk.) Proceed to freeze this in your ice cream maker. When that is done, it's a good time to add shaved chocolate or toffee crunches or roasted almonds or all three.

If I have the stamina to abstain, I like to let the cannister sit in my freezer three to four hours, or even overnight, before diving in. But let your willpower be your guide.

Either way, upon tasting the results, I think you will agree with the French novelist Stendahl, who upon his first taste of ice cream in the 1700s announced, "What a pity this isn't a sin!"

Let the indulging begin.

# Appendix 2

## Sail Away
(Willow's Lullaby)

Music and lyrics by
Billy Sprague
Arranged by
Hardy Hemphill

Where do I    where do I    go when I'm a-

fraid?    Who is there    who is there    lis'-tening when I

pray?    How can I    how can I    cross a stor-my

-2-

Sail Away (Willow's Lullaby)

Sail Away (Willow's Lullaby)

# Notes

**Chapter 1**
1. Loren Eiseley, *The Immense Journey* (New York: Time Inc. 1962), p. 18.
2. Ibid., p. 18.
3. Ibid., p. 141.
4. Ibid., p. 38.

**Chapter 6**
1. Blaise Pascal, *Pensées* (1670), p. 584 translated by W.F. Trotter.
2. Napoleon, *Maxims* (1804–15).
3. Nietzsche, "Notes" (1887), p. 522, in "The Portable Nietzsche," translated by Walter Kaufmann.

**Chapter 13**
1. C.S. Lewis, *A Grief Observed* (New York: Bantam Books, 1961), p. 5,33.

**Chapter 17**
1. Frieda Fordham, *An Introduction to Jung's Psychology* (Viking Press 1966), par. 20.
2. Ibid., par. 20.
3. Ibid., par. 25.
4. Carl Jung, *Commentary on the Secret of the Golden Flower* (Complete Works #13, pars 2–3).

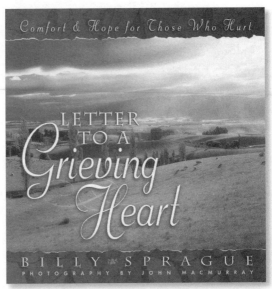

# LETTER to a GRIEVING HEART

## BILLY SPRAGUE
*Photography by* JOHN MACMURRAY

With honesty, compassion, and perspective, Billy
Sprague reaches out as only one who has suffered
deep loss can. Facing the death of a fiancée, a
beloved grandmother, and a favorite college
professor, Sprague pulls from the depths of his soul
to share insights with those living through grief and
heartache. Illustrated with restful, hope-filled
photographs of nature, *Letter to a Grieving Heart* will
comfort the broken and assure them that someday
they, too, will feel the sun again.